Foreword
by the Prime Minister

I am delighted to commend this book about the service of the very many people who contributed on the Home Front during and immediately after the Second World War. Some did so in a voluntary capacity, but all put the nation's interest before their personal safety and concerns. I have heard at first hand, from the Aycliffe Angels in my own constituency, of the sacrifice and hardship endured by all who worked on the Home Front.

This book is written by Lord Briggs – one of our most eminent contemporary historians – working closely with the Imperial War Museum in London.

Today we face different challenges. But the title of Lord Briggs' book – *Go To It!* – is as relevant now as it was sixty years ago. I hope that its story will inspire a similar spirit of single-mindedness, integrity and a desire to serve others as we enter a new century.

Tony Blair

GO TO IT!

WORKING FOR VICTORY ON THE HOME FRONT
1939–1945

ASA BRIGGS

MITCHELL BEAZLEY

In memory of my father, William Walker Briggs,
who exhausted himself in humble but necessary
war work and died at the age of 57 in 1949.

Go To It!
by Asa Briggs

 Published in association with
the Imperial War Museum

First published in Great Britain in 2000
by Mitchell Beazley,
an imprint of the Octopus Publishing Group Ltd,
2–4 Heron Quays, London E14 4JB

ISBN 1 84000 233 6

A CIP catalogue record for this book is available from
the British Library

Commissioning Editor: Margaret Little
Executive Art Editor: Tracy Killick
Project Editor: Stephen Guise
Designer: Nigel Soper
Production: Nancy Roberts

Typeset in Gill Sans and Perpetua
Printed and bound by L.E.G.O. in Italy

CONTENTS

The new Airborne Army is now in action in Europe—equipped by British factories.

THE ATTACK
BEGINS IN THE FACTORY

PRELUDE

MANY OF THE BOOKS about war are epics. They deal with history on the large scale, as Winston Churchill did, and focus on battles and how they were won and lost. Their pages are peopled with war leaders and with uniformed heroes – and villains. There is a place in them, of course, for horror as well as for glory, for stupidity as well as pride, but whatever their bias they are alike in beginning with 'causes' and ending with 'outcomes', victories or defeats.

This is a book about the Second World War – written more than half a century after it ended – that is deliberately different. It is concerned with history on the small scale: with working, not with fighting, and with individuals and families, both in their workplaces and their homes. They were responding to the call 'Go to It!', which provides the title of this book. Most of them had close relatives who were fighting, often far away. The family divided by war is at the heart of the story.

There were heroes within the domestic context, as there were on the fighting fronts, if only because bombs fell on both and civilian casualties could be high. Many of the heroes or heroines were unsung, even in days of bombing – Blitz and V1s and V2s – but there were far more people who were not heroes, 'known' or 'unknown', and who would never have claimed to be. Those in positions of power thought of them as part of 'the war effort', the title of the first chapter of this book, but it is these very people who fill these pages. This prelude and the introductory paragraphs of subsequent chapters provide a necessary framework for their activities, but it is they themselves who constitute the picture.

One of the many illuminating British films produced during the war, usually with government backing, was called *Millions Like Us*. It was a well-chosen title for a Sidney Lauder and Frank Gilliat film that was shown during what at the time was called the 'People's War'. The stars taking part in it appeared as 'ordinary people': Patricia Roc was seen in overalls. Winning the war, it was recognised, depended on full participation as well as on indomitable determination. Not surprisingly, *The People's War* was chosen by Angus Calder as the title of his detailed study of the war published in 1969, itself conceived on an epic scale long after the war was over.

Above The domestic front was often a war of words. Here, in Spring 1943, at an exhibition in Bethnal Green in London's East End, there are posters to be seen rather than goods to buy – or sell.

Nonetheless, 'People's War' was a phrase used at the time with immediate meaning. In 1941, John Marchbank, General Secretary of the National Union of Railwaymen, wrote an article called 'This is the People's War'. 'It is our war', he asserted, 'because the working people have flung their energies into the work of equipping the fighting forces, have surrendered for the time being vital safeguards of normal industrial life, in order that the war trades shall be kept in continuous production and to ensure swift and ample supplies of every essential weapon.'

A book of the moment with the title *People's War* was to appear as a Penguin Special in 1943, although it referred to the Spanish Civil War. It was written by Tom

A Few 'Sung' Heroes

In 1940 Frederick Rose, a maintenance engineer, was one of the first 14 men and women to win the George Medal. In charge of his factory's salvage party, he led workers during an air raid through damaged buildings and, though hampered by flood-water and darkness, personally extinguished fires that had been started among some piles of magnesium.

In 1941 Miss M E White was given the British Empire Medal for remaining alone at her post at the village telephone exchange of Kirby Muxloe, near Leicester, when it was heavily bombed in the late evening. Doors and windows were blown in and Miss White was showered with glass. The following morning she was still on duty, dealing with emergency calls.

Without receiving a national honour, Acting House Foreman George Wilson Cooper of the Great Western Railway was honoured by his company for showing 'great courage and initiative'. With the assistance of his three men, Mr Cooper worked continuously for 48 hours to save 36 horses at a depot that was being bombed with incendiaries and high explosives.

Below *Millions Like Us*, which was produced with official approval in 1943, showed conscripted women on the factory floor (played here by Patricia Roc and Meg Jenkins).

Writing and War Workers

E M Delafield was a female writer who chose to deal with the home front in wartime during the First World War. Her novel The War-Workers *(1918) dealt with women only. It began: 'At the Hostel for Voluntary Workers in Questerham, Miss Vivian, Director of the Midland Supply Depot was under discussion that evening. Half a dozen people, all of whom had been working for Miss Vivian since ten o'clock that evening, as they had worked the day before and would work again the next day, sat in the Hostel sitting-room and talked about their work and about Miss Vivian. Nobody ever talked anything but "shop", either in the office or at the Hostel.'*

The novel showed that in the First World War, as in the Second World War, there could be as much conflict in hostels (and offices) as there was in factories. Delafield added in a foreword, however, that 'the Midland Supply Depot of The War-Workers *has no counterpart in real life, and the scenes and characters described are also purely imaginary'. Writers in the Second World War usually followed suit. They included H E Bates, who in his book* The Tinkers of Elstone *described a Royal Ordnance Factory managed by J Lyons and Company, more famous, as he was, for other exploits.*

Wintringham, who had taken part and was prepared to draw lessons from his experience. Paperback Penguin Specials were very special then: some of them were printed with the words: 'Leave this book at a Post Office when you have read it, so that men and women in the Services may enjoy it too.' I bought my copy of Wintringham in Bradford. I was already in the Army, although working alongside civilians at Bletchley Park.

Twentieth-century wars have often been described as 'total' wars, usually in economic and financial studies of war production, examining what their authors call 'the sinews of war', and written to parallel or supplement studies of 'the fighting front'. The phrase 'total war' was also employed during the Second World War itself, but in a human, not a financial or economic, context. Thus, the novelist E M Forster, at first sight an unlikely source, wrote in his script for the government-commissioned film *Diary for Timothy* (1946) – financial and economic analysis was not in his mind – that 'this was total war. Everyone was in it.'

Below Mrs Vera Elliott of Sunderland, whose husband was serving with the Argyll and Sutherland Highlanders, at her 'first factory job' in May 1941. Note the pertinent poster in the background.

War for Forster was everywhere, 'not only on the battlefields but in the valleys, where Goronwy the miner carries his own weapons to his own battlefront', and in the fields, where 'the farmer [who] has been fighting against the forces of nature all his life… now, with a mortal enemy upon us, has to fight harder than ever'. Working was fighting: they also served who bore no arms.

Total war involved mobility as well as work. Forster's miner and farmer were exceptional in being asked to stay put on the domestic front. They were male, too, while the most striking economic and social change in wartime was the emergence of 'womanpower'.

'The stupendous effort of labour', as the Minister of Labour, Ernest Bevin, described it in 1940, soon after taking office in

Churchill's coalition government, was to reach its climax in 1943, after more than one manpower crisis, and to involve the conscription of women: all women up to the age of 51 had to register. Even so-called 'immobile women', those who could not leave their places of residence, might be called up for national service. One journalist, writing about factory visits in the periodical *John Bull* in 1941, headed his piece 'Put me with the girls' – in block capitals. In the piece itself he talked of 'Bevin's Army'.

There are many photographs of women, and later children, registering before what was always described as 'Call Up', while mobility itself was registered in the fact that there were over 60 million civilian changes of address between 1939 and 1945. The number of telegrams sent increased by ten million each year. The number of telephone calls almost doubled. The Post Office, then a monopoly and always under pressure, had to resort eventually to negative official slogans, similar to those asking people to save fuel, urging families to cut down telephone calls and telegrams.

It was futile guidance. People at each end had things they felt they had to say. 'Is your journey really necessary?' was a more pertinent question. For some of the 'mobile' workers there was a sense of discomfort or – still worse for others – dislocation. For others there was a sense of adventure. It is impossible to generalise as no two families were quite alike in their experiences.

Nor were any two factories, public or privately owned, big or small. Some of them were huge. The quantity of work done there was as striking as its range,

Below The call-up came through inexorably. These young men are registering at a Labour Exchange in late autumn of 1944.

For a healthy, happy job

Join the
WOMEN'S
LAND
ARMY

APPLY TO NEAREST W.L.A. COUNTY OFFICE OR TO W.L.A. HEADQUARTERS 6 CHESHAM PLACE LONDON S.W.1 STREET

Above There were many posters promoting the Women's Land Army (see Chapter 3). A First World War poster, produced for the first Women's Land Army, read 'National Service: God Speed the Plough and the Woman who Drives it'. In the centuries ahead the experience of the two world wars may, however misleadingly, be rolled into one.

including shift work, which involved 'unusual hours', and voluntary work, which continued to play a key role in the civilian war effort, even after a substantially increased element of compulsion had been introduced. Outside the factory the 'battle for production', as it was viewed, was fought mainly on the land, just as the battle for imports, necessary for survival, and for exports, to become more important after the war was over, was fought mainly on the sea. One chapter of this book is called 'In the Fields' — a description rather than a slogan — and despite the peacefulness of the land compared with the 'cruelty' of the sea, many of the women working in the fields were members of the Women's Land Army.

Nonetheless, within the overall pattern of work, it was housework that remained at the core: 'Keep the home fires burning.' Housewives were 'the force behind the fighting line'; and since many older as well as younger women preferred all kinds of work outside the home, part-time as well as full-time, to what they were expected to do inside it, much of the work they had carried out before 1939 was now done by men, particularly older men. Indeed, older men probably did far more housework, often reluctantly, than they had ever done before. The domestic division of labour was changing. Meals too were being served at unlikely times. As much was happening on 'the kitchen front', therefore, as in the canteen.

Good Housekeeping included an article in 1943 called 'Danger — Men at Work'. It began calmly enough: 'Through force of circumstance men are today having to do housework. They do it ponderously and reluctantly, but still they do quite a lot of it'. As the article went on, any sense of calmness was lost. Some of the men had ideas about what they were doing, like changing the shapes of cups and plates to make washing up and stacking easier, but their vision did not stretch to dishwashers. Indeed,

Poster Design

'A designer never chooses his client or subject… it is no accident that in wartime the poster in Britain rose to a very high point simply because every designer could contribute wholeheartedly to a cause, the audience was immediately responsive to the mood of the hour and appreciative of good design, and almost the sole user of the poster in those days, the government, was eager to accept these designs, and encouraged their production. A combination of a cause, a receptive audience and a sympathetic client resulted in [a] fire burst of poster design.'

Abram Games, 1960

Left The well-known
politician FW (later
Baron) Pethick-Lawrence
making jam at his home
in Surrey in 1942.
Pethick-Lawrence had
been a strong supporter
of the Woman's Suffrage
Movement and, with his
wife and Emmeline
Pankhurst, had been sent
to gaol in 1912. He was
a backbencher during
the Second World War,
but became Secretary of
State for India in 1945.

there was a more sophisticated discussion of the relationship between machines and work in the factories and fields than there was in the kitchen – or sadly, where it was most needed, in the mines.

No doubt an abundance of evidence concerning family as well as individual experience is still hidden away in letters and diaries. Some have been published, such as *Mrs Milburn's Diaries* (1979) and *Nella Last's War: A Mother's Diary, 1939–1945* (1981); the latter, like Naomi Michison's *Diary*, was a product of Mass Observation. 'Watching people' and keeping careful accounts of what they saw was its mission. Other unpublished diaries, some with very funny passages, are deposited in the Imperial War Museum. That by Elsie Whitemore and Kathleen Bliss, working in an aircraft factory in South London, had as its entry for 3 November 1942: 'Today was a real Factory Whoopee... Our Managing Director, whom we have never seen before, gave a party during the dinner break, in honour of "two famous pilots" who were coming to see the factory and talk to the workers.'

We want to read on, and we quickly catch the immediacy. There was colour there, as there was in the posters (*see* 'Poster Design', left), not the monochrome that went with monotony in much war work. It is fortunate that so much paper has survived, for people in general were encouraged during the war to throw away, in the interests of salvage, their 'magpie hoard' of postcards and letters and every kind of personal paper, including clippings and bills (if not recipes: these multiplied). Waste was

The Three Salvageers.

Above This Strube cartoon stresses the importance of salvaging. Children were among the most active salvagers, although much of the material salvaged was never used in the war effort.

Below Ernest Bevin talking to Miss Ruby Loftus at a Royal Ordnance Factory in 1943.

anathema. In consequence, more than windows were blacked out. There was restricted scope for taking family snapshots. Newsprint, too, usually printed in black-and-white, was limited.

Because of this – and in the absence of television – films are the most important visual sources for the historian of the Second World War, along with photographs. The latter include both the 'official' photographs of the Ministry of Information, an unpopular wartime innovation soon scrapped when war ended, and press photographs, which were also censored. They should be supplemented by cartoons, which were more difficult to censor at the time. Newsreels must be looked at again also, but they are more revealing for their triumphalist approach and their often condescending style than for their propagandist (and highly selective) content. This sometimes provoked ironic laughter – even backchat – in the dark of the cinemas, which were attended by bigger crowds than ever before.

The best places to find non-official photographs include *Picture Post*, an exciting weekly with political points to make in the text of almost every issue: after the war it did not long survive the advent of television for the millions. *Illustrated* was less exciting, but contained more facts and was equally useful; and older periodicals like *The Sphere* included regular features on the home front, some of them very well written, as well as pages of photographs difficult to reproduce after 50 years. The photographs and many of the words in this book, official and unofficial, come mainly from the voluminous archives of the Imperial War Museum, which also hold posters, an invaluable source, with a significant variety of ways of expressing the same message. The vision depended on the designer involved. One brilliant example, Abram Games (*see* p12), an 'official designer', often found it difficult to please the authorities. One of his 'Your Britain' posters – 'Fight for it Now!' – was removed on Bevin's orders from a poster exhibition.

Official posters drove out many of the pre-war commercial posters from the hoardings, but wartime commercial black-and-white advertisements in the press are themselves of relevance in every chapter of this book: they often took their themes from wartime situations. The advertisements and the posters were said at the time to be 'going to war'. So were official war artists who were already famous, including Henry Moore, who produced many memorable pictures. One showing miners – he came from a mining district — is reproduced in this book (*see* p63). The artists, including Dame Laura Knight (*see* below), were quickly transformed — as artists had been during the First World War — into 'war artists'. They were even granted a special petrol allowance. Many of them on their travels were inspired not by battlefields but by factories, warehouses and shipyards.

Professional entertainers, many of them well known to the public, such as Evelyn Laye, George Formby and 'Stinker' Murdoch, were also sure that they were carrying out important war work, whether they were broadcasting or appearing in person before soldiers, sailors and airmen or — and this was the real novelty — factory workers. Given the shortage of newsprint in wartime, radio was the dominant medium for both information and entertainment. The British Broadcasting Corporation (BBC) was itself censored during the war, if only with what might be described as 'silken cords'. The numbers of people working in it — 5,000 in 1939 — increased dramatically during the war, reaching a peak of 11,500 in March 1944.

The Germans, directing their propaganda at the British, had a 'black' radio station called 'Workers' Challenge', which first went on the air in July 1940. It did not appeal to workers, although it made the most of deep-rooted class antagonisms. Instead, as a then member of British intelligence, Leonard Ingrams, suggested during the Battle of Britain, its most avid listeners were 'old ladies in Eastbourne and Torquay', spellbound because it was using 'the foulest language ever'.

Left Laura Knight: *Ruby Loftus screwing a breech-ring (1943).* This picture is based on a photograph from the same series as that seen on the previous page. Knight, the first woman to become a full member of the Royal Academy (in 1936), was also to paint the Nuremberg Trials.

The British government put out millions of words directed at the so-called 'Home Front'. Many of them took the form of slogans, like the one popularised in 1940 by Herbert Morrison, then Minister of Supply, later Home Secretary, which I have chosen as the title of this book. It was also the title of a BBC programme. Most of the slogans — and jingles — emanated from either the Ministry of Information or from separate ministries — the chief of which were Food, Fuel and Power, War Transport and Health. There were radio 'flashes' too. Some ministries were more imaginative and, just as important, more sensible than others. The same applied to politicians.

Co-ordination was often difficult, as it was in war production where there was no straight equivalent of the Minister of Information, and where there was more than one change, not only of title but also of responsibility. Churchill himself was much too interested in the whole war effort to allow anyone else to be in overall control of what happened in fields and factories and on the sea. Under pressure from Parliament he appointed a Minister of War Production, Lord Beaverbrook, in 1942, but when after a fortnight Beaverbrook resigned for health reasons, Churchill chose as his successor Oliver Lyttelton (later Lord Chandos), whose department was called simply Office of the Minister of Production. In March it became the Ministry of Production. Lyttelton stayed until the end of the war, turning what he referred to at the beginning as his 'so-called Ministry' into an effective agency for co-ordinating British production and American imports.

Lyttelton worked well with Bevin, but was far less well-known by the workers in the factories on which this book focuses. Bevin spoke, as most of the trade unionists did, in his own unmistakable accent, which was very different from those of ministers like Lyttleton. There was a major difference in experience too. Bevin knew that more hours of work did not necessarily mean more work, although they meant more overtime pay. War workers did not like just to be told what to do. They responded to fair treatment and they needed to relax. At the factory level, thereafter, Bevin gave his personal support to two of the best-known wartime radio programmes: *Workers' Playtime*, live entertainment provided in canteens during shift breaks — John Watt of the BBC called it 'a big hook-up' — and *Music While You Work*, introduced in June 1940, which aimed to help 'lessen strain, relieve monotony and increase efficiency'.

This was still a time when leisure was sharply separated from work, more sharply than welfare and entertainment were, and no one would have judged footballers or cricketers by their work effort as players themselves and their managers now do. Yet Gracie Fields, heroine of the cotton towns — or at least until she married an Italian — deserved to have been so judged. The lives of entertainers were profoundly affected by war on every front. Thus, Vera Lynn, 'Forces' Sweetheart', also appeared before workers' audiences. The Entertainments National Service Association (ENSA), always conscious of the fact that it depended on entertainment workers, had an important part to play in the war years, as it never ceased to point out. But so too did classical musicians, who for the first time learned how to perform before factory audiences, sometimes in full orchestras, but more often as instrumentalists and singers.

Alongside ENSA was CEMA — initials flourished in wartime as much as slogans — the Council for Encouragement of Music and the Arts. The latter did not appeal to Beaverbrook, but it offered art and music, as CEMA put it, 'for the people'. As a writer in the *Contemporary Review* explained in 1942, 'the belated discovery had been made that art [and he should have added music as he did in the title of his article] is not the privilege of the few but the birthright of the many'. This was the language of war.

Whatever else went 'unsung' during the war, 'Let the People Sing', an early J B Priestley invocation, was more than a slogan. Music was everywhere, and Priestley himself did almost everything but sing. There were twists, however, to the story of the popular song 'Be Like the Kettle and Sing'. The now 'classic' BBC entertainment programme, Tommy Handley's *ITMA*, featured a song based on Fuel and Power propaganda called 'Polly Take That Kettle Off'. When the BBC tried to ban 'anaemic and debilitated vocal performances by male singers' they did not get far.

Below Vera Lynn, the 'Forces' Sweetheart', was popular with factory workers as well. Her songs created a link between men and women serving abroad and their families at home.

Morale was not a word to be heard much on the factory floor. Nor, indeed, did it figure prominently in the main official wartime publication *Manpower*, which dealt with manpower and womanpower; this was a carefully illustrated brochure of 60 pages, 'the story of Britain's mobilisation for War', which was jointly prepared in 1944 by the Ministry of Labour and National Service and the Ministry of Information. Supplemented by a White Paper in November of 1944 on *Statistics Relating to the War Effort of the United Kingdom* and by a post-war summary Paper of 1951, *Statistical Digest of the War*, it is essential informative reading. By 1951, the war was already fading into the background. In 1944 it seemed a necessary part of the war effort to tell both the British people themselves and Britain's allies (especially America) how great the national achievement on the home front had been.

Between June 1939 and June 1944 the number of men and women in the armed forces or in industry had risen by 3.5 million, or nearly a fifth, and nearly half the total number of women of working age were employed in the women's services, in full-time civil defence or in the war industry. In terms of war production, between September 1939 and June 1944 British shipyards had produced over 700 major war vessels, over 5,000 smaller naval craft and 4.5 million tons of merchant shipping, while

Below 'Go To It!' was not only a national slogan, it was also used by industry. This poster directly related working to fighting, as did 'The Attack Begins in the Factory', seen at the very beginning of this chapter.

by the end of 1943 the aircraft industry had turned out 88,000 planes and munitions factories nearly 24,000 tanks and over 3 million machine guns. Steel production had risen by nearly 2 million tons between 1939 and 1943 and the output of British agriculture had risen by 70 per cent. The acreage of land under the plough had increased from under 13 million acres in 1939 to over 19 million in 1943. The White Paper of 1944 ended not with land or industry, but with people.

> *The vast re-organisation of the British economy... has been carried through in particularly difficult living and working conditions. For five years men and women have lived and worked under complete blackout... Production has been made more difficult by the dispersal of factories to frustrate the air attacks of the enemy... training new labour to unaccustomed tasks.*

Meanwhile, *Manpower* had concluded with a short paragraph, shot through with pride, called 'By Mutual Agreement', summing up the late wartime approach to what it called 'the story behind all our war stories':

> *We could never have survived at all if we had not mobilised our manpower, if the people had not been willing, and, indeed, eager, to grant the Government vast new compulsory powers, and if the Government had not been willing to accept so grand a responsibility. We could never have survived as a Democracy if the colossal task had not been undertaken and achieved in a certain spirit... We have opened a road, which other peoples may wish to travel too, that may yet lead from national cooperation in total war to similar cooperation in the full productive use of resources and manpower in the coming peace. Thus, the manpower story is not only the greatest of our war stories but also something more than a war story.*

To what extent hopes for peace were realised – and those are discussed briefly in Chapter 10 of this book – is a major theme for a very different book. Nor does this book itself claim to be the full story of manpower, which is usually dealt with administratively in terms of shifts of policy and quantitatively in terms of aggregates.

It need not be. The big story is made up of clusters of stories, related or interconnected. *Go To It!* is neither an economic nor a social analysis. It deals with the 'real lives' of individual men and women, when possible illustrated, stripping from their stories what we now recognise to be propaganda, a word that was used in Britain far more at the time than I had realised when I first started to write this book. Having lived through the war, I associated propaganda then with Hitler, Mussolini and Stalin. I was right to do so, but having been involved in recent years in *History Workshops* (the right word in this context), and listened to people reminiscing about themselves, I conclude that there is much that needs to be stripped away, including nostalgia.

Much official war-time 'propaganda', like commercial advertisements, dealt with 'types' rather than with 'individuals' and with models rather than with real flesh-and-blood people. Even when I have little contemporary autobiography to help in my interpretations, I have tried to get at people 'as they were', not in the mass but in

Right Photographs of British workers making uniforms are rare. This German photograph of a tailor's shop, every bit as posed as any British example, shows uniforms, stitched by Singer sewing machines, that are far from battle dress.

particular settings, unfamiliar to them and now recalled as being as different from what came after as from what came before. I have concentrated on various branches of the war effort: munitions, without which the war could not have been fought; food, which kept people alive; coal, on which almost all industrial activity depended; transport, which was essential to make anything or anybody move; and textiles, one of the many problem industries of the pre-war years, which contracted further in years of war and which remained a problem industry in the years afterwards.

Having been brought up in a textiles area of the North of England, I could never write 20th-century history without bringing it in. I was brought up to believe that

Napoleon's armies, in a war longer than ours, wore uniforms made not far away from where I had been living. All the British uniforms of the Second World War were made in Britain. Likewise, most of the German uniforms were made in Germany (*see* left). And their pictures of tailors and soldiers were as revealing as any pictures of ours.

Health and welfare have always interested me. During the war they were central, not marginal, to the war effort. One poster bore the words 'How to keep well in war'. It applied not only to servicemen and civilians, men and women, but also to children. Less attention has been paid in the subsequent writing on the war to the role of children, which had then begun changing. Evacuees are, of course, a great exception, including those who crossed the Atlantic, and have told their own stories. Old people, some considered past working, have been relatively neglected. Some died during the war, some survived it. Experts at the time talked much of the implications of an ageing population, but not of the lengthening of the lifespan, or of the baby boom that would follow the war.

There was much else that we now take for granted that was not foreseen, although there was no doubt about the importance that would be attached to building after the war. Builders do not figure much in this volume, but they are shown in many of the illustrations constructing, and equally important, repairing. They were called upon to build factories, some of them huge, as well as camps. They were a substantial labour force, and there was a degree of urgency about all their work. It was fully appreciated at the time, moreover, that after the war the demand for housing would be a major concern in social policy. As early as October 1940, the *Journal of the Federation of British Industry* was writing that 'bombs have made builders of us all'. Five years later, when the aluminium that had been vital for the aircraft industry was being converted into pots and pans (and even houses), builders were in universal demand (*see* p120).

There were many developments during the war that affected not only places and conditions of work, but also hopes and plans for the world after the war. The shaping of that world was to depend on the people who had lived in Britain throughout the war, the men and women in the Forces who returned to it, and on the children brought up in war conditions. Chapter 9 places them in juxtaposition to people who remembered and had often served in the First World War. The latter had not found the country to which they returned the 'land

Below Shepherd Fred Mitchell, an acknowledged hero of the fields, of Abbots Leigh, Somerset, was awarded the British Empire Medal in 1941 for bravery in saving his flock when fire spread in the lambing sheds.

fit for heroes to live in' that they had been promised. J B Priestley was one of the most powerful voices encouraging them to ensure that history would not repeat itself.

There could have been no other suitable way of ending this book than with a chapter called 'Victory at Last', although it deals more with private victories than with national victory and it does not pretend that 'victory' itself ended everything for families or for the nation. Demobilisation of men and women – the return home – was faster than mobilisation had been, but converting war industries into peace industries was often difficult in times of shortage both of materials and of dollars to buy them. Austerity did not stop in the summer of 1945: with the end of Lend Lease (the arrangement for the transfer of war supplies from the United States to nations whose defence was considered vital to that of the United States), without which Britain and its allies could not have fought the war, it hardened further. The large-scale Labour victory at the general election of 1945 (democracy at work) meant that formal political consensus was over. Whatever opposition there had been since 1940

Factory Workers Can Be Heroes Too

'Thousands of women in the North-East risked their lives daily making bombs and bullets on England's own front line during the war. Some were killed and others lost fingers, eyes and ears in explosive accidents at the huge munitions factories in Aycliffe, under constant threat of German bombings. All worked in extremely dangerous conditions, sometimes through air raids.

Yet they have never even been represented in Remembrance Day parades. No one lays wreaths of poppies in memory of those who died. None of them has ever been awarded a medal.

Today, however, the Northern Echo launches a campaign to win recognition for the women, known as the Aycliffe Angels, who returned home to rebuild their lives with husbands and families after the war, only for their work to be quickly forgotten.

We know that this campaign has, sadly, come too late for those Angels who are now dead. But it is not too late for Maisie Whitle and others like her, many now in their eighties and nineties, who deserve some public recognition for what they did.

We are calling for these women to be awarded the Civil Defence Medal, which a host of war workers including fire guards, nurses, those in the entertainment and even canteen services are entitled to. A spokesman at the Army Medal Office us that Aycliffe Angels were not considered because they were only factory workers. We know they were more than that. We could not have won the war without them.

Many of these women, some of whom are in wheelchairs or walk with the aid of sticks, have told us they long to take part in Remembrance Day parades. We want 1997 to be the year Maisie and her former colleagues can walk side by side with other veterans in the North-East. Let us make is a year for them to remember. Let us assure them we have not forgotten.'

from the Northern Echo, *25 March 1977*

to Churchill's coalition government – and there was more outside Parliament than in it – there had been enough unanimity within it to influence directly post-war policy making and administration. There was also a shared promise of 'full employment'.

One of the coalition government's commissioned wartime films had shown the Arsenal football team with one of the most famous football managers of all time, George Allison, demonstrating 'what teamwork means in football and in war production' – a case of 'British United'. It was not possible to maintain national unity after six years of total war, but for all the renewed thrust of party politics there was more general agreement about 'the way ahead' than there was in most Continental European countries, where sharp differences had threatened the wartime 'underground'.

Go To It! looks back on all of this, but the timing of this book, which is published more than 50 years after the end of the Second World War, relates both to the past and the present. An enterprising and much quoted provincial Northern newspaper, the *Northern Echo*, published in Darlington, campaigned for three years in the mid-1990s, while there still seemed to be time, to pay tribute to those people in County Durham who 'did their bit during the War, only to be ignored afterwards' (*see* left).

One of them, 77-year-old Jennie Harrison, told the newspaper – and the Prime Minister – that 'we lost our youth working in the munitions factory [the Royal Ordnance Factory at Aycliffe] just like the boys who went to war.' 'After all these years,' she went on, 'the country should hear the story.' It will.

Other Aycliffe Angels, as they were called, contributed their personal stories to the *Northern Echo*, among them Mrs McGannon of Bishop Auckland, who stated that at 'the tender age of 17', as she put it, she had been 'the very first person to be employed at ROF 59 as we knew it'. Another correspondent of the *Northern Echo* had worked at the huge Royal Ordnance Factory at Chorley in Lancashire, which figures prominently in this book.

Some of the personal stories of Aycliffe, Chorley and other places can now be told, and an exhibition held in 2000 in the Imperial War Museum played its part in their telling. This book accompanied it but was not designed as a guide to its contents. It cannot examine all the stories in depth, but it traces some of the relationships that lie behind them between memory, myth and history, facts and dreams. That is the stuff of the history of the 20th century.

Below This photograph of Mrs Janet Jackman, an Aycliffe Angel, travelled across Europe with her husband, who became a POW. On working with live ammunition, she wrote, 'nine times out of ten you pressed the filler head down and it could give a nasty bang, you checked that you still had your thumb or finger, in place on your hand… I don't think we really understood the danger we were really in… In retrospect I know now'.

BACK UP THE FIGHTING FORCES

THE WAR EFFORT

HE WORD 'EFFORT' is directly related to the word 'work', noun and verb. Churchill preferred the emotive word 'toil' when he coined the slogan that incorporated both fighting and working: 'Blood, Toil, Tears, Sweat'. During the Second World War there was often as much sweat, sometimes as much blood, even more frequently as many tears, on the Home Front as on the fighting fronts. And there was always toil. When the BBC proposed in September 1942 to launch a new programme 'The British Worker and His Wife during the War', Bevin suggested that the cosy title should be changed to 'Labour's War Effort'. It eventually was broadcast as *The Voice of Labour*. That is how Bevin thought of himself. He often referred to the workers he met in war factories as 'mates'.

During the Second World War the two fronts, fighting and working, were not as far apart from each other – thanks largely to radio – as they had been during the First World War, when 'Blighty' was a very different place from the Somme just across the Channel, or from Mesopotamia, far away. King George VI, for whom it was a personal trial to speak on radio, linked the two together when he claimed that 'each task, each bit of duty, however simple and domestic it may be, is part of our War'; and it was Churchill who told the country that 'the front line runs through the factories'. There were plenty of 'unknown warriors' there. The fact that the war extended after 1941, and became a world war against Japan, as well as Germany and Italy, influenced the way in which the war effort, part of a British Commonwealth effort, was perceived by the people and, indeed, motivated by the propagandists. Perceptions and motivations were similarly affected when the United States and the Soviet Union became Britain's allies.

Above This unusual American poster, which was produced before the United States entered the war, directly related American production to Britain's war effort. Without Lend Lease that effort would have been difficult to pursue.

The British Worker

When Ferdynand Zweig, a Polish professor from Cracow in Poland, wrote his Pelican book The British Worker *in 1952, the word 'war' did not figure in his index. Nor was there any reference to Bevin. There was one revealing remark in it, however, about war itself. 'Patriotism is reserved almost entirely for times of emergency and war: in peacetime patriotic phrases are regarded as traps.' 'There are fifty million people to care for the country's needs', one man told him, 'and there is only one to care for mine'. Zweig, whose earlier book* Labour, Life and Poverty *(1948) had a preface by William Beveridge, one of the great names of World War II, considered the response characteristic. 'But all that changes in times of emergency', he went on, 'and the greater the emergency, the greater his [the worker's] readiness to give his "blood, toil, sweat and tears"'.*

Zweig, a social psychologist, avoided statistics, drawing his conclusions instead from 75 selected case histories, some of them of ex-servicemen. He liked to deal with individual people but he included no women, although in all wartime accounts of the British economy it was 'women power' that figured most prominently. 'You want a million women, Mr Bevin', ran one headline in The War Illustrated *in 1941.*

HUNDREDS OF OUR
GIRLS ARE IN
JAP HANDS

Hate is not enough
WORK *TO AVENGE*
THESE CRIMES

Left The extension of the war to Asia introduced a new dimension to factory propaganda.

Below Mrs Roosevelt receives a 'rapturous welcome' in November 1942 when she visits a Ministry of Supply filling factory in the Midlands.

More has been written about the long-term effects of the wartime sense of a 'common cause' on British hopes and expectations than its immediate effects not only on total output, but also on individual and family motivations – what has been called the 'ethic of work'. War did not figure in Patrick Joyce's book *The Historical Meanings of Work* (1987), yet work on the factory floor was essential in all the countries involved in the War. As film star James Cagney put it in 1942 in a broadcast to 'dear Adolf', he was speaking on behalf of 'all the guys with grease on their faces, who know what work means'. In Britain, workers spoke for themselves. Thus, in the same year, a number of working women sent their own message to President Roosevelt. It was a message of thanks for American Lend Lease materials on which Britain depended, but it was a message of resolution also. In reverse, Mrs Roosevelt visited England to thank the women of Britain for their contribution to the war effort.

Far right, top
This appeal issued in 1941 by the Ministry of Labour and National Service follows 'Marion' from 'manicurist' to forewoman at a munitions factory. It is interesting to compare this official advertisement with that in chapter 2 (see p38), which states of its subject 'Manicurist yesterday – to-day [sic] makes shell cases'.

Happy Birthday Mr Roosevelt

When Roosevelt celebrated his 60th birthday in January 1942, a message was sent to him by Ethel ('Doll') Brown, a factory worker and wife of an Army private serving abroad:

'On behalf of my fellow workers of Britain I have been asked to send you our very best wishes for a happy birthday and to thank you for the help and encouragement which you have given to the workers everywhere.'

Mrs Brown was speaking from the stage of His Majesty's Theatre in London during an ENSA concert. She was wearing a 'butcher-blue overall and navy slacks'. Her last words were 'We shall keep together until victory is won and in the days of peace to come. God bless you.'

According to a Daily Sketch reporter, Mrs Brown, when asked about clothes replied, 'Well, I haven't bought much since the war. I put what I can into War Savings.' The reporter, a woman, Elspeth Grant, described Mrs Brown as 'just about 5ft 6in of the salt of the earth'.

Morale, usually called 'spirit', always counted during the war, and after the war ended, 'the Dunkirk spirit' was often invoked. If people had worked so hard in times of war, why could they not work equally hard in times of peace? There were many personal examples. *The War Illustrated*, which printed many photographs of women at work, included one of Evelyn Duncan who had set up a world record by turning out 6,130 anti-aircraft shell components in six days. Once the war was over, illuminating

Far right, bottom
A German poster asking French workers to join their factories and help win the war against Bolshevism.

Are you equal to two German women?

Two of Them to Every One of You

'Your opposite number in Germany has spent her year in a labour camp. Her limbs are strong, her stride is firm, and her spirit is uplifted by a perverted idealism. She labours willingly, passionately, indefatigably, in the shipbuilding yards and the heavier industries, for one end – the glorious defeat of Britain and the triumph of Nazism. For the men over military age are not enough, two million enslaved Poles are not enough, the Italian arsenals are not enough, to feed the German war machine… if Britain is to be humbled and crushed. So the German women pour out of the kitchens and into the factories… Two of them to every one of you.'

details of other women workers were published: at the Ford Works in Dagenham, dedicated to war production, Lilian Rowe, once head of a kitchen department at a Lyons Corner House (a popular restaurant during the war), was picked out for breaking all records on one shift.

It used to be claimed that Britain made more use of woman power in wartime than Germany, but it is now clear that the proportion of women in the German workforce remained higher than that of Britain throughout the war. Nonetheless, what can still be correctly claimed is that British attitudes towards women's work were very different from those in Germany and were depicted differently by British and German media. There were some British workers who resented the influx of women, particularly in small factories, just as there were others who objected to the 'dilution' of skilled labour. But they were in a minority, and as a trade unionist, Bevin was able to shape policies that he knew would command official trade-union support. Before he had taken office at Churchill's request, Bevin had been at pains to win the support of the Labour Party and trade unions and had travelled down to Bournemouth, where their conferences were being held, to secure it.

On 22 May 1940, when Churchill was preoccupied with the last stages of the war in politically divided France, the momentous Emergency Powers (Defence) Act passed through all its parliamentary stages in three hours. It gave the government, in the words of Clement Attlee, leader of the Labour Party and the man who was to become Churchill's Deputy Prime Minister, 'complete control over persons and property, not just some persons of some particular class of the community, but of all persons, rich and poor, employers and workman, man or woman, and all property'. On the afternoon of the same day, Bevin was empowered by Regulation 58A 'to direct any person in the United Kingdom to perform any such services as he might specify'.

This was compelling language, but it was not until 1941 that words gave way to deeds. An Essential Work Order came into force in March by which Bevin acquired the power to declare work carried out in any establishments to be 'essential'. The most important of these were establishments in engineering, aircraft production, shipbuilding, railways, mining and the building industry. Managers could not dismiss workers without the consent of a National Service Officer; workers could not leave their jobs without permission.

By the end of 1941, some 1,000 firms were on the Register of Protected Establishments kept by the Ministry of Labour and, as part of the changes, women had to be registered, eventually up to the age of 51. There was still a projected 'manpower deficit', however, leading to the conscription of women in December 1941. It was recognised by then that

a 'manpower budget', covering all kinds of work by both men and women, was as crucial to the winning of the war as a fiscal budget. As Chairman of a Manpower Requirement Committee appointed by Bevin in August 1940, William (later Lord) Beveridge, who was to become famous for his report on social security in 1942, had emphasised the importance of such budgeting.

The existence of mass unemployment of pre-war years was in the background of both manpower planning and social security legislation. In the 21 years between the First and Second World Wars, there were never less than one million unemployed and, during the last months of the so-called 'phoney war' between September 1939 and May 1940 the total unemployment figures, still standing at over a million, had actually gone up. It was abundantly clear by then that there would be a growing demand not only for soldiers, sailors and airmen, but also for skilled workers to produce aeroplanes, tanks, rifles and shells. Yet at the end of March 1940 there were only 7,000 people in Government Training Centres, a necessary part of any manpower strategy. Britain really only began to 'roll up its sleeves' in June 1940, after the fall of France.

The war effort, which ironed out some of the divisions between different parts of the country, with their varying records of employment and unemployment, demanded both improvisation and organisation. It was impossible, however, to carry through many fundamental structural changes in industry: in the organisation of coal mining, for example, dealt with in Chapter 4, and this despite political pressure from miners to have the industry nationalised and their unwillingness to abandon restrictive traditional work practices.

In the case of aircraft production – on which the fate of the air Battle of Britain depended in 1940 – Lord Beaverbrook, the Canadian owner of the *Daily Express*, was given full powers by Churchill to ensure that fighter aircraft would be ready as quickly as possible. As is shown in the next chapter, 'Waste Not a Minute', he put improvisation first, but it would have been impossible to keep up for more than a limited amount of time the frenzied effort Beaverbrook demanded both from others and from himself.

In later stages of the war, when the way to victory became associated, correctly or incorrectly, with massive air power and with the production of bombers, not fighter planes, there was less emphasis on improvisation than on organisation. This had always been the case in engineering and in building. It seemed to Bevin that there had to be control as well as drive. Thus, in the industry which he knew best, sea transport, he secured a National Dock Labour Scheme. Dockers' tardiness in loading and unloading ships was a matter of complaint, even of anger, to Canadians and Americans, as were wartime strikes. To Bevin they seemed likely to continue until dockers, treated as casual labourers before the war, secured what they themselves considered to be social security.

Bevin also won an impressive majority in Parliament (285 votes to 118) when he introduced a Catering Wages Bill, ensuring collective bargaining in that scattered and largely non-unionised industry in January 1943.

The Pressures in 1940

From a record kept from May to June 1940 by E A Platt, who worked in a Birmingham factory before leaving in 1941 to join the Royal Air Force.

'Everything seemed to happen so quickly during this period – the Spring offensive of the Germans was so successful and Dunkirk was upon us very quickly. From one of the top floors of the factory where I worked… we gazed in awe and sympathy and many more emotions as every train pulled in with its consignment of returned soldiers – some wounded – in all types of clothing – even pyjamas! And everyone must have said there [sic] own silent prayer to God for the miracle – and all the effort everyone connected with the evacuation had put in.

We were all then made to understand, quite clearly, that we "stood alone" against the aggressors. I believe that the old saying "England's last hope" came into everyday parlance. The rumours during the Summer months were quite out of this world… every day on assembly lines we listened to gory stories from "someone" who had a letter from "someone" who lived "somewhere on the East Coast"… – "German bodies washed up with the tide" – "Navy has set fire to the North Sea" –…

It all added spice to everyday working life – and upon recollection – these rumours matched any "duff gen" dished out in the RAF whilst I served.

There was, however, a feeling of impending doom… surely one of the first "nerve-mass" on a nation's population – it was a case of living "day-to-day"'.

The aggregate figures relating to the war effort have been given in the Prelude. They were impressive, although they have since been placed critically in long-term perspective. By themselves they explain little. Behind the aggregates individual motivation even in wartime was not simple. Shirkers were condemned, as were 'spivs', but 'too much work' could be suspect: there were still 'restrictive practices'. Higher wages than before the war were an important incentive – as were the increased possibilities of overtime – despite the fact that there was a shortage of consumer goods and that taxes were high, with far more people paying them. Whether women's wages should be equal to men's was often a matter of keen argument: pamphlets and articles were devoted to the question.

Much was made of comparisons with Russia. In propaganda terms it was not American workers – or those speaking on their behalf – who most appealed to British factory workers, but Soviet workers who often hit the headlines in the press. With limited consumption and the cutting out of all fripperies, all the emphasis was on record-breaking production. The 'Stakhanovites', who, following

Below Workers at a Midlands tank factory show their support for the Soviet Union with two Valentine tanks destined for delivery to the Red Army

Above and top Caribbean workers joined the British work force, though only in small numbers. Indian workers were also a presence in the factories, although far more Indians served in the Forces, making a substantial contribution, than as part of the civilian labour force.

the pre-war model of the coalminer A G Stakhanov, broke all work records, attracting much attention. There were so-called Russian 'two hundreders' and even 'thousanders' who were held up for 'socialist emulation'. Yet outside the munitions industries Soviet productivity fell during the war below its low pre-war level, and whatever the headlines in both the *Daily Express* and the *Daily Mirror* might say — and they were often in tacit collusion with each other in focusing on the Soviet Union and its workers, as well as on its soldiers — it was the United States that set the example.

Only in retrospect did Britain realise that it was the United States that provided the model. *Picture Post* certainly did not make this plain at the time, nor did Ministry of Information propaganda. All agreed, of course, that Germany was the land of 'slave labour', dependent, as the war continued, on foreign workers from occupied Europe, millions of them, who for the Germans were very far from being 'millions like us'.

In Britain there were many official wartime photographs of British workers, all subject to censorship, which showed them being visited by royalty, by politicians, by foreign leaders — and in war factories by generals and by men in the 'front line', particularly airmen and tank crews who used the products made by the workers shown in the photographs. (The first censors were said to have been disturbed when they learned that their blue pencils were made in Bavaria.) Most often, war workers were depicted being told how the products which they had made were actually being used. They were sometimes given demonstrations, but the workers themselves were part of them.

Help from Overseas

Among the 'labour force' there were many Irishmen, arriving both from North and South, some 40,000 of them finding employment in the munitions industries.

A small new element that became familiar only in the post-war years was West Indian. Three groups of young West Indian trainees were brought in to Government Training Centres in the North-West, where West Indians were already working in munitions factories. One famous and familiar West Indian personality, the brilliant cricketer, Learie Constantine, was already known and admired by Lancashire crowds.

There were also timber workers from British Honduras and Newfoundland. They were followed by groups of Indians, most of whom, after studying at Government Training Centres, were sent home to India to work in munitions factories there. They were a witness to the fact that this was a world war with an Asian as well as a European fighting front.

Montgomery's Shock Brigade

Joan Lambert, the editor of the War Service Bureau run by the widely read Woman *magazine, drew the right lesson. Referring to a Win-the-War contest organised by the London Women's Parliament for factory workers and housewives in the London area, she described how the first prize for the 'brightest industrial team' was won by the Montgomery Shock Brigade in a shell-making factory in Surrey. The team sent General Montgomery a cable to celebrate their win. They had reduced lateness by all clocking in on time, cut down absenteeism, and increased production. Their target for shells for the first week was 9,000: they produced 9,187. In the second week they produced 9,538, and during the third week they produced 10,312 shells.*

Such targeting was common and often took the form of a contest. As Joan Lambert noted, in every factory it was the trained workers who set the standard and broke the records. There were special features, however, in the Montgomery team: they believed in training women to operate all machines, so that in case of sickness or absence, any operator could take over any machine. They also had first-class women tool setters who kept the machines in good running condition, such as Mrs Skeats. After one of the workers had met with a slight accident Mrs Skeats sent her over to do a lighter job, took over her machine and turned out a record output.

Mrs Loveday, who organised the contest for the Montgomery Shock Brigade, was 50 and had been a munitions worker in the last war. She could turn out 40 shells an hour – a 'better score' than that of many of the younger women.

As in the Soviet Union and the United States, it was mainly munitions workers who were on show. Less publicised were the railway workers on whom both factories and furnaces depended, as did everyone in uniform, although in a war of slogans and jingles the main transport posters called railways 'the lines behind the lines'. A new ministry called the Ministry of War Transport was set up in 1941, headed by businessman Frederick Leathers, a railway and shipping employer who got on well with Bevin. One of their many official reports was called 'Transport Goes to War'. Everything was said to be going to war, including buses, barges and carthorses.

Left General (later Field Marshal) Montgomery, always known as 'Monty', visited war factories as a part of his duties, both when he was in North Africa and in Europe. Here he is seen talking with Charlie Taylor, an 85-year-old factory worker, in 1944.

Nonetheless, this was a war effort with only limited mechanisation and primitive electronics, a word not then invented. There was 'operational research', but no computerisation, except in cryptography. Scientists engaged in war work, 'boffins', were kept from view. Their work was secret. It was not until 1941 that the British Press gave details of the existence and characteristics of radar; and it was not until years still later that the achievements of Bletchley Park ('Station X') were made known. There, hidden from view, civilians, some of them very young, worked together with men and women in uniform. Only Churchill was in a position to recognise how critically important their work was to the war effort.

The development of jet propulsion, conceived before the war by Frank (later Sir Frank) Whittle, faced formidable difficulties, and there was only one type of jet engine ready for service in 1944. Meanwhile, the successful, if from the start controversial, work on the atomic bomb, in which British scientists played a major part, was not revealed until the first bombs had been dropped on the Japanese cities of Hiroshima and Nagasaki in August 1945. The project had to be developed in Los Alamos, New Mexico, because Britain had neither the financial resources nor the manpower to pursue it on British soil.

On this side of the Atlantic voluntary effort, painstaking and often imaginatively conceived, was extolled at a time when most expert work had to be kept secret, and it continued to be extolled after an increased measure of compulsion had been introduced by 1942. The grandest of its organisers, Lady (Stella) Reading, founder of the Women's (later Royal) Voluntary Service, who has still not been granted the biography she deserves, wrote without rhetoric that 'we have learned [through war] that it is no good talking about things, we must do them… We have done work we

Above A rare group photograph, privately taken in 1945, of civilians and members of the forces who worked together at Bletchley Park ('Station X'), the headqaurters of the British cryptographic effort that played a key role in the winning of the war. The group consisted of members of Hut 6 (Cryptography) and Hut 3 (Intelligence). A number of Americans also worked at Bletchley Park from 1943.

Work in Secret

There was a university atmosphere at Betchley Park. Rank mattered little. Nor did whether or not you were a civilian, a soldier, an airman or a naval officer. There was a military camp at the other side of the Park perimeter, but its Commandant did not enter the premises. The rules of secrecy prevailed absolutely and were faithfully kept by almost everyone working at Bletchley. There were far more women than men, many of them in uniform, and this gave a distinctive tone to the establishment. Social life flourished – and with it gossip – but it was the intensity of the work, and its urgency, that bonded people together. The buildings that surrounded the Victorian house were new, and the people who worked in them, some on what would now be called 'computers', kept their secrets to themselves.

never thought to have to approach and we have carried burdens heavier than we knew existed.' This chapter follows her in trying to get behind rhetoric – and propaganda – to muscles and skills, to deeds, not talk – or, for that matter, ideas – while recognising that there were other aspects of the total war besides 'effort' that have to be understood if the history of it is to become 'total' too.

The distinctively British combination of voluntary effort and compulsory service, unique in its pattern, did not remain constant throughout the war. It has to be charted, therefore, preferably in detail, occupation by occupation, region by region. *En bloc* 'reserved occupations', recognised as being essential to the war effort in 1939, were dropped in 1941, the year that women's conscription was introduced after efforts to mobilise voluntary women's labour had proved inadequate. In the same year recruitment for 'civil defence', a matter for pride, ceased to be voluntary also. Post-war television programmes, such as *Dad's Army*, often repeated, keep the first phases of the war alive.

On the first Sunday of the war, in Oxford, Lord Nuffield, automobile manufacturer and benefactor, who owned the great Cowley Works, coined the slogan 'Work and Pray' – Chamberlain's solemn speech announcing war was delivered on a Sunday morning – and *The Sphere* in June 1940 showed pictures of London workers 'giving up their Day of Rest', as Morrison had urged them to, 'in order to speed up output'. Hours of work, divided into shifts, remained long and exhausting throughout the war, but by 1943 a more appropriate slogan would have been 'Work and Play' (indeed, J B Priestley would have preferred this in 1940). Chapter 8 on entertainment explains how 'entertainers' advanced their argument that they (or at least some of them) were essential war workers.

During the last two years of the war, savings, always a theme for propaganda, were being canvassed more than salvage – children were the liveliest propagandists in both cases – and there was a gradual running down of some of the munitions industries. By then, too, how to prepare men and women in the Forces for civilian work was a major preoccupation within the context of demobilisation rather than mobilisation. The 'war effort' in the factories had reached its peak in 1943. It deserved praise, but more than 50 years later it demands discussion as well as recollection and celebration. In some respects it left Britain less prepared for years of peace than its enemies.

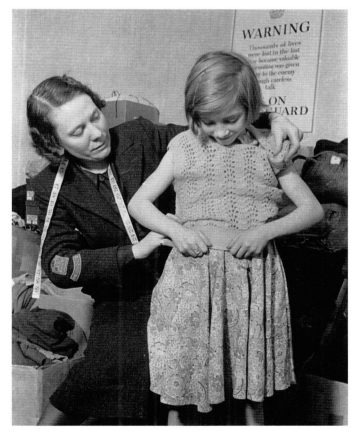

Below A jumper that came 'all the way from America' pleased this little girl so much that she is said to have forgotten the horrors of the previous night, when her home was destroyed and she lost all her clothes. She is watched over by a WVS worker.

WOMEN OF BRITAIN
COME INTO
THE FACTORIES
ASK AT ANY EMPLOYMENT EXCHANGE FOR ADVICE AND FULL DETAILS

2

WASTE NOT A MINUTE

WAR FACTORIES were sometimes described as 'arsenals of democracy'. For most of the people working in the least efficient of them this must have sounded like a bad joke: they were neither arsenals nor democracies. Yet the making of armaments, including aeroplanes and tanks, was crucial to the success of the democracies on the fighting front and there was often urgency in the demand for them. Some factories responded magnificently. 'Yield not an Inch! Waste not a Minute!' Churchill, who remembered the shell crisis of the First World War, called munitions 'the raw materials of victory'. No fewer than 3.5 million people were employed in manufacturing them in 1943, the peak point in the manpower statistics. Their importance had been fully acknowledged during the period of 'phoney war' before Chamberlain gave way to Churchill, when there were no fewer than 16 'campaigns' to sustain morale. A well-illustrated article on 'Shells' in *Illustrated* in October 1939 took up the theme of war production more or less where it had been left off in 1918. During the First World War there had been a woeful shortage of ammunition. Now the lesson had been learnt:

When an Illustrated *cameraman visited a munitions factory… he found everything working with clockwork regularity that suggested shell-making might have been going on for years.*

Significantly 'only a few short months' before, although rearmament was under way, this particular Black Country factory had itself been a shell.

There was more talk of bombs than of shells in 1939 and 1940, and there was more than a touch of romanticism in a 1941 article in *Picture Post* called 'Making a Beautiful Bomb'. It claimed that bombs were moulded 'as if they were designed to please.' In fact, as the war went on relentlessly, bombs became increasingly more destructive, and no reporter would have called them beautiful in 1944 or 1945.

By then there had been three great production 'drives': for more aircraft, more tanks and more ships. In relation to the first of these, emphasis was placed less on beauty than on accuracy. 'Propellers must be perfect'; 'meticulous accuracy is called for at every stage of the intricate manufacturing process.' There was still no shortage of rhetoric, even when there was a shortage of materials. 'The tip of an aeroplane's propeller whizzes round at a velocity of 680 mph during each flight. At that dizzy speed the pull on each blade of a bomber propeller is as great as it would be if the blade were loaded with seven double-decker buses.'

In shipbuilding, emphasis was placed on new techniques like 'prefabrication', introduced from the United States. The industry now employed large numbers of women as riveters, welders and painters, although it was still bedevilled by conflicts between unionised crafts that had nearly always been there behind the scenes even when British shipbuilders were leading the world. The riveters earned

Above Advertisers had their own advice to offer war workers, particularly women (see p84 for another in the series).

Left Women were less imaginatively used in shipyards, as seen here, than in aircraft factories. They took the place of men only in non-skilled work. The caption to this photograph states with some exaggeration that 'no job is too big for them. Electric welding, riveting, painting, electric wiring and French polishing are just a few of the skilled trades in which women are lending a hand.'

Build the Ship

The praises of women shipyard workers were sung in V S Pritchett's official booklet Build the Ship (1942), which also presented an idealised picture of men at work, particularly in the forges and the platers' sheds. In the former, common to most industries, 30 or 40 blacksmiths – with three helpers each and a boy – worked, each man standing before his hooded fire, his face smoky and reddened by the flame and glistening with sweat. In the latter, distinctive to shipbuilding, it was not individual people but 'groups or gangs' that were important. The author of the booklet waxed eloquent when he described the welders: 'When they tip back their masks or helmets, they look like nuns or knights, and reveal that medieval aspect of modern industry which is confirmed by the sight of collective work.'

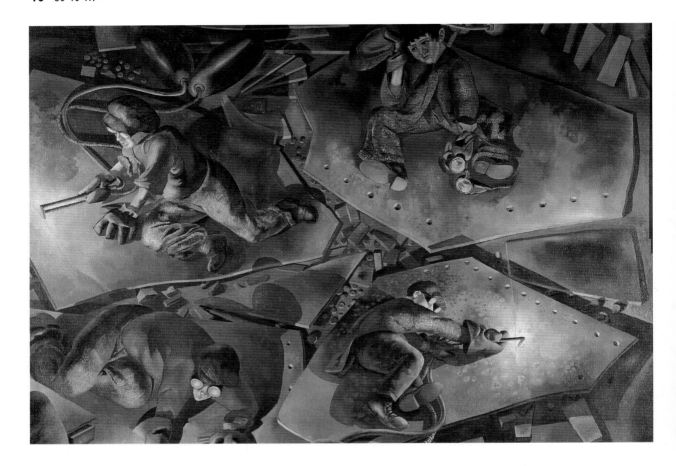

Above Stanley Spencer: *Shipbuilding on the Clyde: the riveters* (1944). Spencer made his shipbuilders timeless, but the 'fusillade of the riveters' is now a forgotten sound.

the highest wages. Now after years of unemployment the industry faced a big test. It had been an industry with workers insecure about jobs and with owners insecure in face of foreign competition. Both workers and owners carried their insecurity into the future.

War meant that all berths in the shipyards were full. There were now only two customers – the Admiralty and the Ministry of War Transport, both of them concerned with productivity and speed, neither of which could be guaranteed. A ship's officer who visited a highly inefficient shipyard at Liverpool in 1943, engaged in repairs, was appalled by the sight of idleness. He was quoted in a book by J L Hodson, published in 1945, *The Sea and the Land*:

> There's a group of [workers] always to be seen in the bottom of a hold round a brazier. What they're supposed to be doing, I don't know. They're never working when I see them. A Government official who accompanied me said... "Just take a look as we walk round and see if you discover anybody working." He added that he visits these sorts of yards from time to time, and the sight makes him almost weep. He estimates (somewhat satirically) that the men working are one in ten.

This judgment was frequently repeated in the future. And idleness did not exorcise unrest: there was a record number of strikes. Nor did an injection of capital investment, the first for many years. A Shipbuilding Development Committee, set up in 1942, spent £6 million in the following two years. There was no radical restructuring of the industry any more than there was in mining. Few individual records survive. The memories do.

Merchant shipping, on which the future of Britain's food (and fish) depended, captured most of the public attention. Prefabrication not only made building easier, but simplified repair, yet it was often resisted by a management that was afraid of innovation. In the middle of the war, an official committee headed by industrialist Robert Barlow found in the shipyards 'an atmosphere based upon an inadequate appreciation of the urgency and gravity of the National situation' as the country was waging a continuing 'Battle of the Atlantic'. 'In some cases,' Barlow added, 'the Management appeared content with the existing position.' They did not wish, in face of union opposition, to dilute the labour force. The proportion of skilled workers in the industry, highly demarcated, did not change greatly during the war. It was 50 per cent in 1940 and 45 per cent in 1945. By then the volume of British shipping, necessary for export recovery, had fallen by 30 per cent.

The story of tanks was different. In 1942 and 1943 the spotlight played on aid for Russia. Earlier it had played on the deserts of North Africa. 'How a filter beat the Libyan sand' was one headline in *The War Illustrated* in March 1941, which described how C G Vokes, an inventive engineer, had devised a filter that would enable tanks to travel 150 miles a day 'without the least trouble from sand'. In one filter factory the workers had refused to take off two hours before Christmas in 1941 to spend shopping. 'We don't want the time off,' they are said to have replied. 'We'll shop later on. We've a job of work to do.'

In 1942 all eyes were on the Russian front, and 'Tanks for Russia Week', which began on 22 September, has passed into history. All tanks then were to be sent to the east, speeded on their way by Beaverbrook, advocate of a 'Second Front', and by Ivan Maisky, the Russian ambassador. In 1942, its peak year, British production of tanks reached 8,600. Their names were historic – 'Crusaders', 'Cromwells' and 'Churchills'. The industry, however, was scattered about in various factories, large and small, and Germany was ahead in tank production to the end. Its peak year was 1944 when its comparable figure was 19,000. Meanwhile, Britain itself depended on tanks from the United States. Supplies of American tanks to Britain between 1939 and 1944 exceeded those produced by Britain.

Aircraft production, which in 1940 was given its separate highly unorthodox Ministry under Beaverbrook, produced 'miracles' before the Battle of Britain in the

Below A British poster makes effective use of a Russian counterpart to promote efforts to send aid to the Russian front.

SOVIET WAR POSTER

ДВЕ КРЕПКИЕ, КАК СТАЛЬ, РУКИ
ДРУГ К ДРУГУ БРАТСКИ МЫ ПРОСТЕРЛИ.
ОНИ, ВРАГА ЗАЖАВ В ТИСКИ,
СОМКНУТСЯ НА ФАШИСТСКОМ ГОРЛЕ!

TRANSLATION
TWO HANDS IN FRIENDSHIP, STRONG AS STEEL,
ONE TO THE OTHER ARE EXTENDED.
THE FASCIST THROAT THEIR GRIP WILL FEEL
THROTTLING TILL LIFE IS ENDED.

Rush British arms to RUSSIAN hands

Above This long-range photograph of Hurricanes in construction concentrates on what is being produced rather than on the worker or producers. It is designed to bring out the scale of production.

Right When the Minister of Aircraft Production, Lord Beaverbrook, told housewives in 1940 that their pots and pans were virgin aluminium he was more than 99.2 per cent correct. The first 50,000 kitchen utensils collected in response to Lord Beaverbrook's appeal went into the furnaces. They are said to have come out as ten tons of pure aluminium, worth, then, £1,100.

autumn of 1940. For example, a small factory in Birmingham, which manufactured all the carburettors used in Spitfire and Hurricane fighter aircraft, doubled its weekly output in less than a fortnight. This was a critical time, when the public was being urged to get rid of all aluminium pots and pans and turn them into Spitfires and Hurricanes. Among those who subscribed financially to a Spitfire campaign were Durham miners, who provided funds for three. This was more than propaganda, and the Women's Voluntary Service (and the schools) who collected pans discharged their mission with zeal. Later in the year, there was no need for propaganda behind the drive to produce machine guns for fighters after the Birmingham Small Arms factory had been hit by German bombers. There was urgency then.

Production problems remained throughout the war. As in the case of tank production, the industry was dependent on sub-contracting and on what the official historian of war production called 'stubbornly persisting small workshop methods'. Not even the appointment of Sir Stafford Cripps as Minister of Aircraft Production in the autumn of 1942 (a political demotion for him) solved the problems, although he set up a Production Efficiency Board and, at the factory level, encouraged Joint Production Committees that he frequently addressed.

Women workers were by then making a major contribution to mass aircraft production, which in 1943 employed 1,750,000 men and women. Photographs, official and unofficial, showed women fitting engines for Stirling bombers, riveting bomb floors and erecting gun turrets. Of the Mosquito bombers that they helped to make it was said not only that they went out to bomb Berlin but that they could also fly to Russia and back in a day. On the organisational side, by 1943 over half the engineering

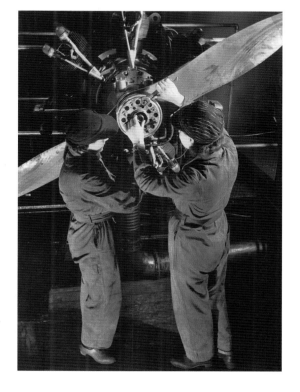

Below Women played an important part in aircraft production.

factories were carrying out some aircraft work, with the large firms that employed more than a thousand workers contributing half or more of their war effort to the making of aircraft parts.

Sociologists from Durham University have recently studied the Aycliffe factory and found that many of the women working there had never worked before. It was 'a massive place you got lost in easy', one of them recalled. Another said that the first impression it gave was that of a prison 'even on a nice day'. Those who adapted best might become 'Blue Bands': overlookers or 'seniors' who supervised work as well as doing it. The foremen, however – there were few forewomen – sometimes treated 'a pretty face' as a 'measure for promotion'. Others told women working there that 'if you knew what you were carrying you wouldn't do it'.

The Chief Inspector of Factories, high among officials, had given good advice to women war workers entering an engineering factory for the first time:

"Going on Duty".

Above A Randolph Schwabe illustration (c.1946–47) for HE Bates' account – *The Tinkers of Elstow* – of the Royal Ordnance Factory managed by J Lyons & Company. The girls were wearing different kinds of overall: there was no uniform.

The first week in a large works is very like the first week in a new school. You will be in strange surrounds and will find yourself among a busy set of people, all of whose work has to be carefully arranged in order that the finished article may be turned out quickly and well. Your first friends will be your FELLOW WORKERS. If approached in the right way, you will find them willing to help and show you the ropes. They will help you to learn your way about and give you useful tips on your own particular job, on what to do and what to avoid; do not be afraid to ask them. You will soon discover the friends who are most willing to help.

Your next friends will be your CHARGEHAND AND FOREMAN OR FOREWOMAN. These are very busy people, but you will find they are ready to help you with the details of your work and they are not of the severe type that was common in my young days. Next to a good workman, a foreman loves a good time-keeper. Remember the foreman has a kind of jig-saw puzzle to complete each week and your absence will upset that puzzle, so avoid unnecessary risks of injury or ill-health. In this connection, may I advise you to think of the importance of your own particular piece of work, even if it is the making of one small part over and over again. Your pieces are designed to fit into the whole.

In a *Picture Post* article written earlier in the war called 'They make the guns we need', J B Priestley had concentrated on male workers, describing an enormous Ministry of Supply factory where you could not see the whole of the main shed from either end. 'The atmosphere was that of Vulcan's cave.' It was the workers and not the work itself that most interested him when he paid his visit. They were employed in two shifts, not three, and the work never stopped. The factory was a contented place, in Priestley's opinion, for three reasons.

First, it was government owned: 'everybody there was in the same boat, being all state employees'. Second, 'the management ran the place on easy but not free-and-easy lines'. This was 'industrial democracy, and not the remains of feudalism imperfectly adapted to industry'. There were no 'fancy jobs'. Third, 'these people were earning very good money'. They were almost all on piece work and they were working exceptional hours.

The last point matters. At another Ministry of Supply factory, 'somewhere in the Midlands', Ron Hubble, a worker who made anti-aircraft guns, worked a 67-hour week for £8, earning 'twice as much as I ever had before'. He was one of the few male workers to be named. In the 1930s he had earned 25 shillings a week in an artificial silk factory, ten shillings of which had gone on rent for a four-room house. The account in the Press of the factory where he worked should be compared with a fictional factory described by Priestley in his novel *Daylight on Saturday*. This was a place where 'three in the morning and three in the afternoon look[ed] the same. Nothing tells you the difference except the rhythm of work.'

The factories in which women and men workers were employed varied significantly not only in size, but also in age, location, industrial relations and 'atmosphere'. The variations were pointed out at length in a Mass Observation report of 1943, *People in Production*, which chronicled a wide range of workers' and managers' attitudes. Bevin was highly critical of the approach to this in what to him was an unhelpful report, which suggested that things were seriously wrong and that 'the people in production need[ed] pulling together'. 'The goal [was] common, the desire to co-operate', but there had been an 'accumulation of ill will from the past' and far too much was being left to the individual firm. Government was not giving the necessary lead.

In fact, it was trying to do so. The most famous of all armaments factories in England in 1939 was Woolwich Arsenal, 'the father of all British munitions factories', an arsenal resonant with history. Some of the other 43 publicly owned ordnance factories in 1945 were brand new, such as Nottingham, which began production in 1937 and worked at full pressure throughout the war, turning out 13,000 guns of various calibres, and 23,500 gun-barrels. It had a monthly quota of 330.

The various government factories had diverse products and were very different in scale. Blackburn specialized in fuses and rifle components; Birtley in cartridge cases and in components of the Bailey bridges that enabled troops to cross almost every river. Each factory was proud of its own identity, as well as its carefully targeted output. Without the individual factory being mentioned, the names of specially identified

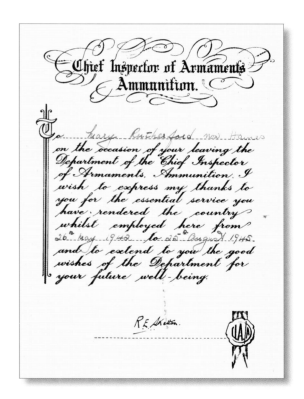

Above Mary Rutherford's official Leaving Certificate from the Chief Inspector of Armaments. These certificates were often kept and greatly treasured.

A Memorable Record

'If the workers in the Power House and Blast Furnace were deserving of the epithet Bravest of the Brave, those in the other parts of the factory were scarcely less worthy of praise. They regarded themselves as an essential unit of one single organisation, Britain at war, of which a part was manned by the men who drove the vehicles they made and another part by those who fought the combats they witnessed daily during the summer of 1940 above the factory where they worked. This was demonstrated in various ways, but in none more striking than in the efforts the workers made to reach the works. Though their houses might have been destroyed and their families rendered homeless, and sometimes worse, they did their utmost to arrive on time, despite the fact that many lived considerable distances away.

Walter Flight, for example, travelled daily from Lewisham to work a 12-hour shift. One day in September 1940, after witnessing the death of one of his colleagues an oil bomb exploded in the factory, he set off at about 7am to return to his home. He reached it to find it in ruins and his wife and child unhurt, but much shaken in their Anderson shelter. That day he evacuated them to Dorking, returned to his duties, and henceforth slept in the factory until the attacks died down the following year. Then he returned to his patched-up house, only to lose it altogether in 1944 by blast from a flying bomb which injured his wife and child, who had by then returned. But he never lost a day's work.'

from Ford at War, *Hilary St George Saunders (1946)*

workers were sometimes focused upon. Thus, in May 1942, Mrs Edith Foster, who was 'a leading hand in charge of fourteen girls at one factory', was singled out as a representative of all war ordnance factories in a new series of BBC programmes called *Award for Industry*. Her husband was serving abroad in the Army, and they had one baby daughter.

In January 1939, a huge new Royal Ordnance Factory began production at Chorley, 21 miles north of Manchester. It covered 1,000 acres and was built 'according to plan' and not to meet a 'wartime emergency'. It was soon known to employ more new wartime workers than any other factory in Britain: there were between 35,000 and 40,000 of them. Each day no fewer than 76 trains stopped at its railway station, conveniently placed on a main line. The factory was also served by 500 buses, and some of the workers came from as far away as Liverpool and Blackpool. Security was tight; the gates were guarded by the War Department Constabulary, and every worker had to show a pass.

Once inside, workers quickly became familiar with its clean and dirty areas, straddled by a shed known as 'Shift House', where they were required, if moving into the 'Clean Area', to put on white, closely tied, buttonless overalls, white woollen skull caps for men or turbans for women, and nail-less shoes. They were searched by a character whom Ian Hay, historian of the factory, called an 'elderly Cerberus'. Every worker had to know how to handle TNT. In the early days, it was rumoured, some innocent workers had used sticks of it as chalk. Most of them obviously learned fast. The wartime death total of 134 was not to be dismissed, but given that there had been in total 350,000 employees at Chorley, some of them only briefly trained, it was surprisingly low.

In most factories there was a danger zone and in many of them there was a Welfare Department. At Woolwich the women, who worked there were in the charge of Mrs Miriam Moon, who had been in the Arsenal for more than 20 years; she was described in 1940 as 'the only woman to hold such a position of danger and responsibility in any British ordnance factory'. By 1945, however, women had been promoted to similar posts, with a few of them becoming eloquent recruiters of new labour (before conscription was introduced).

Among them was Vera Elliott, born in Sunderland, who made tyres for heavy army lorries, and whose husband was a lorry driver in the Army in India. She addressed large meetings of women (sometimes 3,000) in her 'spare time'. One of her favourite locations were big department stores, but she also spoke through a megaphone from travelling vans. Another 'persuasive' woman public speaker was 19-year-old Betty Wilkes, who made bomb components in

Far left Margharita Haines, a 21-year-old ex-model and dancer, widow of a DFC pilot who was killed in action, explains her work to a glamorous Duchess of Kent at a Ministry of Aircraft Production aero-engine factory in 1941. When the Duchess asked her if she liked her work she replied that she loved it: 'I feel that I'm doing something to finish the war'.

I'm only a wartime working girl,
The machine shop makes me deaf,
I have no prospects after the war
And my young man is in the RAF
    K for Kitty, calling P for Pure...
    Bomb Doors Open...
    Over to you.

Night after night as he passes by
I wonder what he's gone to bomb
And I fancy in the jabber of the mad machines
That I hear him calling on the intercom
    K for Kitty, calling P for Pure...
    Bomb Doors Open...
    Over to you.
    'Swing Song', Louis MacNeice (1942)

Above Workers at a Ministry of Supply tank factory chalk their greeting to Hitler on the side of a finished tank. Not all such greetings were as polite.

her factory. She had once been bombed out of her own home.

The word 'propaganda' was not a bogey word in such circumstances. Indeed, an article, 'Internal Factory Propaganda' in the *World Press News* in February 1942 stated with pride that 'some of the most attractive propaganda today is being carried out in the large individual plants in various parts of the country… mostly by… advertising messages and publicity offices'. It went on to mention Fort Dunlop, the huge rubber factory where Harold Eleg, advertising manager, was chairman of a highly successful War Savings Committee. He was also committed to 'production drives' that made use of 'posters, wall newspapers, slogans, displays and so on'. At Fort Dunlop output had increased and absenteeism diminished.

The author of the article described another Birmingham factory that used among its slogans 'Work like hell and give Hitler the works'. Hitler's telephone number was given as 'Double Cross 40' and his telegraphic address as 'Atrocity'. The underlying slogan, which covers the whole of this chapter, was less imaginative, 'get on the target and join the attack'.

One privately owned factory, very different from Woolwich, Chorley or Aycliffe, occupied the upper floor of John Perring's store in Kingston. Between 1942 and 1945, volunteers were hard at work on making munitions. The Perring contribution had started in 1942, when the directors of Hoover Ltd, makers of vacuum cleaners – and thus a household name – encouraged the setting up of a number of 'satellite' factories making parts of aircraft. At the Staines branch of Perring's, six volunteers started work in 1942 on war production; by 1945 there were 1,200. The factory still looked like a store and the works office, wages department, girls' restroom and canteen kitchen were housed in the peace-time 'show flat' on the first floor. One of the volunteer workers at Perrings of Kingston was 44-year-old housewife Bertha Martin, whose husband Bert was serving with the Royal Army Service Corps in Italy. In the words of the company's well-illustrated war history:

Perhaps the most striking feature to a visitor was the atmosphere of cheerful zeal. Chatter! – of course they chattered – from morning till the end of the day. They sang too – with a will – for these were free women fighting for their own liberty, volunteers working with their hands and their hearts, producing the weapons needed to back up their own husbands and sons in the front line. And whilst they chatted of food difficulties and clothes coupons and children's ailments and the latest letter from abroad, and as they sang and laughed the work went on and 15 tons of cables were transported into and out of the Staines premises in a week. Between 1942 and 1944, the cable preparation for the complete electrical equipment of 1,400 Halifax and Lancaster bombers was the contribution of these enthusiastic ladies.

The Kingston store, starting later, produced more than 8 million coils. No fewer than 450 miles of wire were used daily in five production units. The slogan here was 'The Schedules Must Be Maintained'. It was not so much a slogan, perhaps, as an injunction that lay behind all the efficient sectors of the nation's war effort.

Below A cricket scoreboard was among the more imaginative ways of informing workers how they were confronting targets – but note 'Quality First'. How strong its appeal was to women workers then is less certain. Nor were the two men on the right of the photograph workers on the shop floor.

3

IN THE FIELDS

'Food is a munition of war,' ran one of the many wartime slogans, 'don't waste it'. An even more famous and far more positive slogan was 'Dig for Victory', sometimes shortened, as in a popular song, to 'Dig, dig, dig' and applied to all forms of war effort.

There were, in fact, two types of wartime slogans: those concerned with the land and those concerned with the kitchen and the canteen. The word 'food chain' had not yet been invented, but its meaning would have immediately been plain. Inevitably, transport came into the picture: 'Let your shopping help our shipping.'

Lord Woolton, who became Minister of Food in April 1940 while Neville Chamberlain was still Prime Minister, knew how to use all such slogans to best effect. In his first broadcast to the nation he set the tone:

> *Last week the Prime Minister did me the great honour of asking me to become the Minister of Food. I hesitated, I doubted my ability to do a job so colossal. I turned to my wife, I thought, and then I took the job – believing that I could rely on the women of this country to help me. We have a job to do together, you and I, an immensely important war job. No uniforms, no parades, no drills, but a job wanting a lot of thinking and a lot of knowledge too.*

Even before that, ration books had been printed and rationing introduced in January 1940, and the women of the country had already been called to duty, to work not on the 'Kitchen Front' but on the land.

Right The Women's Land Army Timber Corps, which comprised 6,000 land girls, prided itself on its efficiency. They carried out many jobs, from felling to sawmill operations; here they are loading trees felled for pit props. In 1943, Britain imported only 25 per cent of the timber needed compared with the pre-war figure of 90 per cent.

Before the war had begun, the Women's Land Army was officially brought into existence at the home of Lady Denman who had served previously with an earlier Women's Land Army during the First World War. By 1943, when numbers of recruits were at their peak, 80,000 women had enrolled. 'Strong, sturdy and weather-beaten', they occasionally staged their own rallies and parades; they always had their own uniform – green jerseys, corduroy breeches, brown felt slouch hats and khaki overcoats; and they also sang their own song.

> *Back to the Land, we must all lend a hand,*
> *To the farms and the fields we must go,*
> *There's a job to be done,*
> *Though we can't fire a gun,*
> *We can still do our bit with the hoe;*
> *When your muscles are strong,*
> *You will soon get along,*
> *And you'll think that country life's grand;*
> *We're all needed now,*
> *We must all speed the plough,*
> *So come with us – back to the Land.*

The song won recruits. The WLA was never 'the Cinderella' – the Forces' poor relation – that the writer Vita Sackville-West, a devoted gardener, called it in her wartime booklet of the same name published in 1944.

Above Gwendoline Finnimore, a 15-year-old shepherdess, rounds up her flock on Exmoor with the help of her two dogs. Conditions of sheep rearing varied in different parts of the country, according to geography and tradition.

'Speeding the plough' and raising cereals were only two of the tasks that the WLA carried out. Like all farmers, WLA members were engaged in a wide variety of jobs. While most of these, such as hoeing and threshing, involved food production, the Land Girls (some of whom had come from the factory floor) might be rat-catchers or thatchers, poultry keepers or shepherds. Most of them were employed in the field and took part in ploughing and haymaking. A sizeable proportion of them were involved in milking – 20th-century milkmaids – dealing with cows at a time when hand milking was giving way to machine milking in 'progressive farms' (trainees in East Sussex learned milking on rubber cows). One milker, Mabel Berry, who was billeted in the house of the local cowman, was responsible for taking calves each week to Havant Market in Hampshire, driving a horse and cart.

Six thousand members of the WLA were serving in its Timber Corps, formed in 1942, felling mature trees, sawing wood, and planting new trees. They wore distinctive green berets, and their employers were not individual farmers but the Ministry of Supply. The fellers, like Kathleen Johnson from Filey in East Yorkshire, were entitled to wear a distinctive brass badge of crossed axes on their armbands.

The Timber Corps

Winnie Catterell from Wigan started work miles away at Horsham, Sussex, starting as a tree-feller and going on to become a 'measurer'. She was responsible for calculating the volume of timber that was being felled and sawn.

In coal mining, no parallel tasks would have been handed over to a woman even in wartime.

Most of them worked with men, including woodcutters from Ireland and Canada.

The varied work of the WLA received generous publicity during the war, with much of it covering particular members of the Army such as Kathleen Johnson. A photograph of her swinging an axe was widely distributed by agencies in very different parts of the world. The best-known and best-connected of them figured in newspaper gossip columns as well as in news stories. There were striking press photographs of weddings, some of them with Guards of Honour carrying pitchforks, rakes or spades. Some publicity centred also on agricultural Stakhanovites, such as a former hairdresser who won a horse ploughing contest in Yorkshire, where all the other contestants were men. Another press photograph that attracted the attention of the agencies was that of a group of workers who had become known as 'The Amazon Squad'. They were shown not at work, but gathered for a 'jolly singsong' round a Land Girl pianist, Rita Clarke.

Some of the women wrote their own accounts, often anonymous, of 'life on the farm'. One of them, an ex-nurse, described 'littering, foddering cows, hedging and ditching, putting in tiles and looking after calves.' 'The farmer's work,' she concluded, was 'work never done'. She enjoyed the sense of continuity in her own work, overlooking the monotony. 'There was a curious, fascinating, total, enduring exaltation which probably does much to explain why farmers so seldom give up the life, despite all their grumbling, some of which is thoroughly justified.'

One typewritten account in the Imperial War Museum, by Mrs V Brown, compares factory life, where she started work at the age of 18 in a Rochdale factory making

Agricultural Training

Wye Agricultural College had to cancel its 'normal' courses and become a Training Centre for Women, even before war broke out in September 1939. The first batch of 80 wartime recruits came from 34 varieties of occupation. Another 111 followed in December. 'It was simply amazing,' the Journal of the College recorded, to watch 'little typists and shop girls forking muck, starting and driving tractors, milking cows, trussing poultry, cleaning pig sties, digging vegetable beds, picking potatoes and sprouts… in wet weather and in fine… mostly wet.' Some of the women being trained, not there but elsewhere, spoke disparagingly of 'so-called training'. But there were centres of excellence.

Later in the war the Ministry of Supply drew attention to a Women's Land Army Training Camp at Culford in Suffolk which offered a month's course for between 100 and 150 women. Others were attached to the Northamptonshire Institute of Agriculture.

Just after the war a seven-week Agriculture Certificate Course was held in Cambridgeshire for the women wishing to stay in the WLA after the war.

packing rings, to life on a farm where she was chased around by bulls and by Italian prisoners-of-war. In the factory, where she worked long hours with 'a good crowd of women', the windows were all blacked out. On the farm the lovely countryside was 'magic'. Her hostel was friendly, six or eight dormitories, 'each holding six or eight girls in double bunks'. The pay was low, however, and when she received her uniform in 1944, she had to surrender clothing coupons for it. She was saving up to get married, and when her boyfriend in the Royal Army Service Corps returned at the end of the war, she had to borrow some coupons before the wedding. The members of the WLA had received no gratuity on leaving it; in fact Lady Denman resigned in protest. Like the Aycliffe Angels (but writing in 1988, 11 years earlier) Mrs Brown felt that the WLA should be represented at the Albert Hall Remembrance Services and at the Cenotaph on Remembrance Sunday. 'I will always have my memories,' she ended her account, 'and I would do it all again if I could'.

Several autobiographical accounts by members of the WLA have been published. Norah Turner called hers *In Baggy Brown Breeches and a Cowboy Hat*; Joan Mant chose

Above Many memorable photographs of the Women's Land Army show a single member leading a flock of sheep or, as in this picture, a gaggle of turkeys or hens.

Right These 'land girls', photographed in August 1941, have their arms full of wheat gathered from some of the 180 acres of wheatfields found on formerly derelict parts of the Sussex Downs.

Below David Caseley, a Devon farmer with 50 acres, pictured in 1942. He increased his milk production during the war and ploughed up, for the first time, a quarter of his acreage. He did not work alone: it was all achieved 'with the help of his wife and their twin daughters'.

as her title *All Muck, No Medals*. They serve to bring out the variety of individual attitudes as well as experiences in an Army that was proud of its corporate identity and in an 'industry' that depended on teamwork. One memorable photograph shows a team of seven 'land girls' bringing in the harvest, which yielded 17 hundredweight of grain per acre, in what was said to be the biggest wheatfield in Britain, high up on the Sussex Downs: it had not been ploughed for 20 years.

Some farmers were disgruntled at the amount of attention which the WLA received. Yet there were farmers who were themselves the subject of Ministry of Information articles and photographs. Among them was 'Douglas', a Cockney evacuee from Barking, who worked for the Holdworth family as a labourer at Hills, Kingston Blount, on the edge of the Chilterns.

There were some newcomers to farming also, including women, who were not members of the WLA, and who felt uneasy about who was being photographed and what was being written. One of them, Betty Shaw, in a note kept in the Imperial War Museum, spoke of both 'happy' and 'hard' times and of the lack of appreciation of her work and of her husband's efforts. 'I always thought our worst enemies were the farmers' wives. The Germans were nothing to some of these'.

Farmers were operating under the aegis of County War Agricultural Executive Committees, bodies possessing wide powers but consisting of farmers. One of their tasks was to draw up a kind of 20th-century Domesday Book. Land was registered and evaluated, like people. The contrast with the present situation in agriculture is striking. There were still 545,000 farm horses in 1945 and, although there had been a marked increase in the use of tractors (some of them operated by women), there was relatively little mechanisation. Moreover, farmers and their wives often felt that what science there was meant 'going against nature'. The use of fertilisers was encouraged, but phosphates and potash were rationed. Ironically, that gave some hitherto uninterested farmers an incentive to buy them.

Agriculture ('farming plus') and food distribution were kept separate from each other during the war, as they are now, but they were united by common interests in the circumstances of war: everyone had to dig for victory. Potatoes provided perhaps the biggest link, as they did between farmers and gardeners. Described by Beveridge as 'puckish vegetables', potatoes were considered both nutritious and easy to grow.

Woolton, who introduced his own recipe for 'Woolton Pie', found the right slogans and jingles to proclaim their virtues, inspiring the lines:

> *Those who have the will to win*
> *Cook potatoes in their skin,*
> *Knowing that the sight of peelings*
> *Deeply hurts Lord Woolton's feelings.*

Fanfares announced Woolton's arrival in December 1942 at a spectacular bomb site in Oxford Street where a Christmas Potato Fair was in progress. It is thought that Woolton himself played Father Christmas at the Fair.

Each visitor to the Fair signed a potato pledge: 'I promise as my Christmas gift to the sailors who have to bring our bread that I will do all I can to eat home-grown potatoes.' Then, laden with hot baked potatoes from Father Christmas and potato coupons, 'exchangeable for extra potatoes at any greengrocer', the visitors continued on their 'calorific way'.

The Women's Institutes (WI) were also zealous advocates of the potato. Their members were told happily in 1941: 'There is no restriction in increasing your potato plot. A few receipts [recipes]

The Wrong Sort

Unusual situations led inevitably to tension. Mr C Copson, a farmer from Rothley, complained at a meeting of fellow farmers at Leicester:

'My two Land Girls wanted to bath before the kitchen fire, and I had to wait outside in the snow. One, a London actress, shouted through the key-hole, "Come in and dry my back." That is not the type of girl I wanted.'

Below This poster, which evokes the call of Chamberlain, speaks for itself. What is less explicit is its emphasis on mechanisation: methods of ploughing were changing.

Potatoes – the nation's iron ration. A record crop is being grown now. Help to gather it in

MAKE SURE OF A FULL PLATE

Mr Middleton

There was one man more than any other who represented the war effort in the gardens: Mr Middleton, never known by any other name. At times he seemed to be running the war on his own. Thus in 1941 in the Daily Express Middleton chose as the heading of his weekly article 'It's Time to Dig In, Mr Middleton gives Orders for the Spring Offensive.' Mr Middleton was also one of Britain's best-known broadcasters, and had his own allotment opposite Broadcasting House. Even window boxes, he told his readers and listeners, could be put to good use. 'No garden? Try a window box.'

using POTATOES TO SAVE FLOUR… are to be found in another column'. In another issue of *Women's Institute News* members were given advice on a different but not unrelated subject (which is also the focus of the next chapter, as are the bitter *Punch* cartoons reproduced there), written from the fireside: 'Do remember that gas and electricity both come from coal, and that by using either you are initially using coal, so use them as carefully as if they were the last two pieces of coal in your cellar on an icy Christmas Eve.'

Interdependence was one of the themes of the Second World War, learnt by citizens as well as workers – the latter often appalled by the hold-ups in supplies. 'Get into the habit of planning your cooking so as to make the utmost use of the heat you turn on. When you use your oven, fill it to capacity, when cooking under the grill, remember to use the heat above'. Most sensible of all, 'think up attractive ways with salads, cold foods and drinks'.

It is revealing that this last advice came neither from the Ministry of Food, nor from the Ministry of Fuel and Power, nor even from the Ministry of Information. It derived from an entirely voluntary body which consisted of consumers, not producers: the WI encouraged keeping pigs too. (There was a piggery as well as an allotment in Hyde Park.) In Werrington in the Potteries members of the WI, in addition to carrying on a 'Grand Jam Drive', were said to have developed corns on their hands as they filled buckets of

In the Allotments

Allotments were popular, and there were 500,000 new allotment holders by 1944. However, in an Economist survey of that year only 20 per cent of allotment holders claimed that they were working them to help the war effort. Fifty-five per cent said that their main aim was to produce fresh food and 16 per cent to acquire fresh air. Nearly 18 per cent said that they wished to save money. Such a combination of public and private interest lay behind much voluntary, and even compulsory, war work.

Far left, top Potatoes became almost sacred symbols of war. Every year there were demands for a record crop. Carrots came second.

food to offer the pigs. It was judged a consolation, however, that 'the pigs were happy if they were not'. Wisely, far away from Werrington, but not far away from Hyde Park, John Winant, the American Ambassador, noted in Grosvenor Square that although it was possible to build a factory in a month, it took a four months to produce a pig, whatever you did, and even longer to fatten it to be ready for slaughter. Before coming to London, Winant, who greatly admired Bevin, had directed the International Labour Office in Geneva.

Emphasis on 'Back to the Land' should not overshadow facts concerning 'Out to Sea'. The Ministry of Agriculture was also a Ministry of Fisheries. With shortages and rationing, diet changed during the war, if not as much as some nutritionists would have wished. It was not only consumption of meat, vegetables and fats that was affected: trawlers, although facing hazardous journeys, benefited from the unprecedented demand for fish. Their catch had greatly increased in value. In 1941 the lowest-paid member of a trawler's crew could make a sum during one trip that could work out at £1 a day, more than the average factory worker. A mate's daily earnings, according to *The War Illustrated*, could average £5, 'while those of a skipper (might) equal the salary of some Cabinet Ministers'.

Whatever else might or might not have become a myth during the war, the pre-war penny herring had already become one. So, it seemed, had the genuinely white loaf that most people still wanted to eat. Instead, when the first peals of bells rang out in 'celebration' of victory in North Africa in November 1942, Woolton, approving of all that was happening on the land, was presented with the winning 'nutritious' Victory Loaf at a display of 7,000 loaves made by British master bakers throughout the country. Baking was one kind of work that had to go on continuously in war and peace (though there were, of course, restrictions during wartime, and fines were imposed for 'permitting bread to be wasted'), and it was only after the war that bread was rationed.

Far left, bottom Allotments were a much publicised contribution to the war effort. This one, with the Albert Memorial in the background, was famous. No mechanisation to be found here; the year was 1941.

Below Land and sea were often inextricably linked in some posters, such as this clever composition.

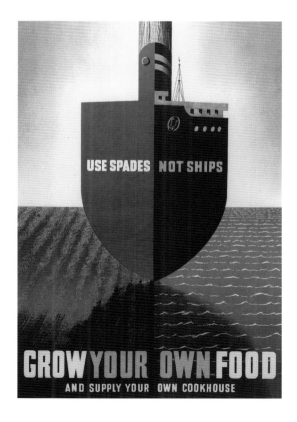

4

DOWN THE MINES

MEADOW AND MINE
"How's *your* harvest, mate?"

Above and below
These Punch cartoons
by E H Shepard directly
relate coal to crops and
coal to fighting. Above, a
farmer asks a striking
miner, 'How's *your* harvest
mate?' Below, the question
put by a soldier is 'When
are you going to put up
your Iron Cross?'

STRIKING IN THE WEST
"When are you going to put up your Iron Cross?"

B RITAIN'S ALL-OUT INDUSTRIAL EFFORT depended on coal, by far the main source of energy for factory and home, as well as for gas and electricity production. The war made people fully aware of this, something they had not been during the years of unemployment in the 1920s and 1930s when mining had languished. They would have been even more aware of it had coal been rationed, but this was never the case. The press – and Churchill – were hostile to it, although most sections of the public would have favoured it. Those who were the most opposed, the better-off, were also most hostile to the men in the pits, as some cartoons revealed (*see* left).

'Coal', wrote Charles Graves in *The Sphere* in November 1942, was 'the life-blood of Britain's war industries.' Until the fall of France in 1940 it was exported across the Channel, but with the end of that market there was unemployment again. There was also a wastage of miners through natural causes: sickness and retirement – and accidents, treated also as inevitable if not natural; although Hugh Dalton, President of the Board of Trade and Member of Parliament for a mining constituency, believed that the main problem in mining was an ageing labour force.

It was always necessary to relate the input of new miners, many of them brought in by compulsion, some brought unwillingly back, to the numbers going out and, as Dalton recognised, their age in both cases mattered when 'productivity' was being assessed. By 1945, only 18 per cent of miners were aged between 25 and 35, whereas the comparable proportion before the war had been 25 per cent. Young men re-directed into the mines in 1943, 1944 and 1945 were often frustrated, and levels of absenteeism rose accordingly.

So too did the number of strikes. More time was lost through them in 1943 than in 1942. In the words of the President of the National Union of Miners, Will Lawther, speaking in 1944, there had 'never been a time when there was such unrest and dissatisfaction in the country's coalfields.' In the same year one miner, Bert Coombes, pushing to one side thoughts of blood being spilt on the fighting fronts of war, wrote in a book called *Those Clouded Hills* (1944): 'There is blood on the coal, there will always be blood on the coal, but we feel that blood should be shed for the men that are our kin not for the enrichment of a few who have battened on our pain in the past'.

The sense of history was strong and the unrest was communal, as well as individual. Miners had always had their own way of life and mining villages were tightly knit communities. A book describing their attitudes and relationships, written soon after the war, was called *Coal is Our Life*. During the war, a South Wales miner, writing eloquently in *Picture Post*, claimed special virtues in coal miners: 'once a man has fought Nature deep in the inside of a mountain he is not afraid of anything that life can do to him.'

When the great war artist Henry Moore returned in thick fog in 1941 to the mining district in Yorkshire where he was born, in order to do drawings of miners at work, he descended into a local pit.

> *Crawling on sore hands and knees and reaching the actual coal face was the biggest experience. If one was asked to describe what Hell might be like, this would do. A dense darkness you could touch, the whirring din of the coal-cutting machine, throwing into the air black dust so thick that the light beams from the miners' lamps could only shine into it a few inches — the impression of numberless short pit props placed only a foot or two apart, to support above them a mile's weight of rock and earth ceiling — all this in the stifling heat. I have never had a tougher day in my life... but I wanted to show... that I could stand as much as the miners.*

When Moore drew his graphic pictures of miners at work (*see* below), he succeeded in conveying the 'claustrophobic effects of countless pit props' and 'the gritty, grubby smears of black coal-dust on the miners' bodies and faces at the same time as the anatomy underneath'.

It did not need a great artist to appreciate that loss of turnover suffered because of technical obsolescence and breakdowns, along with transport problems, was almost as serious to the nation as ageing, wastage, accidents or even unrest. Despite improvements in welfare facilities (including baths — and many mines did not have them) most miners did not feel that they were working in a well-managed industry.

Below Henry Moore: *At the Coal Face: a miner pushing a tub* (1942). On the Continent of Europe the name 'underground' was usually associated with resistance movements. Moore's underground was here and in London's shelters.

The demand for nationalisation, a major structural change, was consequential and persistent. A White Paper on the industry that was produced in 1942, and which won the approval of the House of Commons by 329 votes to 8, was not popular at the coal face even though it introduced 'dual control' of the industry by government and owners – with a National Coal Board – and was followed by generous would-be conciliatory wage settlements.

Suspicion remained, and when the government did not immediately underwrite an award offered to miners by an official tribunal in January 1944 and accepted by the owners in the belief that the government would endorse it, the miners went on strike. Almost 200,000 tons of production were lost in one month, February, the highest such loss during the whole of the war. In total, over 1.6 million tons of coal were lost in the first quarter of the year, and it required a ruling from the Minister of Fuel and Power – David Lloyd George's son Gwilym, who had taken over what was then a new post – to reshape the pay structures and restore industrial peace.

The average earnings of miners were said before the ruling to be placed twenty-third in the list of average earnings of all workers. Miners paid as much attention to such tables as to football league tables: their trade-union leaders chose always to relate their pay to other workers' pay rather than to their own productivity. Their league table, however, was national, not international. In Germany, where productivity was higher, 97 per cent of coal produced was cut by machine when War was declared. The British figure was only 60 per cent.

After the ruling, British productivity and output increased temporarily during the second quarter of 1944, but there were now inflationary dangers given that the price of coal determined most other prices. A young temporary civil servant working with Beveridge, Harold Wilson, a future Labour Prime Minister, suggested in his first book, *New Deal for Coal* (1945), that the problems were more complex than most people realised. While noting that statistics could not record 'the persistent guerrilla warfare which continues in the majority of pits between management and men', he went on to establish that half the 1,700 pits in the country – 466 of them employing fewer than 20 men – were being kept afloat by the other

Below 'Bevin Boys' (*see* p66) at a colliery near Canterbury in Kent, spring 1944.

half. This was a recipe for disaster, as was pointed out in the 1945 Report of a Technical Advisory Committee chaired by Charles Reid, Director of Production at the Ministry of Fuel and Power.

For Wilson, as for others, almost the only black spot on the Home Front during the war had been the coal industry. From the beginning of 1941 onwards, the country had constantly been in danger, but sadly the 'life blood' of Britain's war industries was congealed. Output from deep mines fell from 231 million tons in 1939 to 224 million tons in 1940 and then to 206 million tons in 1941. Output per man also fell.

The sense of insecurity that influenced the government and the country when the supplies of coal deemed to be necessary were under threat was paralleled by a sense of insecurity on the part of the men working in the pits; they had known more bad times than good before the war and were not convinced that wartime prosperity would last. Miners living in different mining districts (in Yorkshire, Derbyshire and Wales) may have undergone different pre-war fortunes, but everywhere there had been industrial strife. It had seemed a necessary part of a grim pattern. What would the future hold?

In 1939, the industry had been in urgent need of heavy capital investment for the replacing and re-equipping of its pits. Owners of pits – and governments – not miners, were responsible for this. The miners, however, were a dwindling labour force. There were 766,000 of them on the books in 1939; by 1942, when the new Ministry of Fuel and Power was established, dealing with gas and electricity as well as with coal, there were 709,000 of them, roughly the same figure as in 1945. In 1941 an Essential Works Order had been applied to the mines, but in the three months following the end of the war, the number of miners leaving the industry was again exceptionally high.

There was a consumer side to the story of coal, expressed in BBC fuel flashes and advertisements. It was a staple of the home as well as of the factory. As in the case of food, voluntary bodies gave advice on how to use it. Thus, the *Women's Institute News* told its readers in August 1944, 'Now is the time to tidy up the coal shed. If you have any coal, coke or anthracite dust left, start right in on making briquettes. Don't leave it until your new deliveries arrive... Aim at getting the utmost

Below In this poster for urban consumers 'private' and 'public' are revealed in a very different confrontation from that in the mining regions.

Above This young miner was not a Bevin Boy. Fourteen-year-olds were still working in the mines, and this one is not using a miners' canteen, which were not usually as good as factory canteens. Disgruntled miners in one canteen left a factory menu on their table after eating their own food.

out of whatever fuel you can for the winter.' The need to save gas and electricity in the home did not require to be reinforced by advice. It was taken for granted. There were good financial incentives for doing so.

Meanwhile, in 1943 Bevin had tried one way of securing miners through his 'Bevin Boy' scheme, which received a great deal of publicity at the time. When insufficient numbers of volunteers for mining were forthcoming, including young men who were opting to go into mining rather than the Forces, he decided to direct men of call-up age by ballot. Only those who were on a shortlist of highly skilled occupations or who had been accepted for aircrew or submarine service were exempted. Bevin hoped that this would secure the labour of 50,000 Bevin Boys in 1944, but in fact there were only 21,000 ballotees (volunteers meant that the total number of Bevin Boys was greater). Few of them reached the coalface, but after training they were responsible for valuable work in underground transport and other operations involved in coalmining.

Some of them were highly articulate and, like members of the Women's Land Army, can best speak for themselves. Two, at least, wrote books. One of these, Derek

The Bevin Boy

'The irony of our training was that we never saw any coal nor did we ever get dirty enough to have to take a daily shower in the pithead baths. The coal drawing areas of the pit were all centred round the other shaft, where loaded tubs were speeding upwards to the surface at a rhythmic pace through the day… Our training accustomed us to going underground, but as far as practical experience of coal mining was concerned we were as ignorant at the end of the month as we had been at the beginning.'

from **The Bevin Boy**, *David Day (1947)*

Left A Bevin Boy, Jim Walters, using a pneumatic drill in a colliery in Kent, one of the few collieries where Bevin Boys worked at the coal face.

Zero Hour for CLE

'This record of how the first air raids on London developed from the point of view of CLE [Central London Electricity Limited] may be of interest to readers now on active service:

We had had our first comparatively slight experience of bombing in the Central London area, when four bombs fell in the City a fortnight before, but, as everyone knows, the real attack started on Saturday, September 7. I happened to be on duty that weekend, and after a long alarm during the afternoon, went up on the roof to have a look round, and immediately saw dense black clouds of smoke rising from the East, lit up at the base by the red glow of flames. This was the fire at the docks which also destroyed many homes in the East End.

Later in the evening there was another alarm and I went up on the roof to have a last look at the fire before going to the shelter, but we did not stay long as we suddenly heard two bombs whistling down and explosions not far away. I had my first experience of that sensation described by "Edgar" as "a covey of partridges flying round in the pit of one's stomach". We got to shelter in quick time.

During the night London was lit up by the light of the East End fires; many of the tall, light-coloured buildings showing up very clearly and making conspicuous targets and landmarks. At 11.30 I was in the front shelter, where some of the ladies were dispensing cups of tea, when the first bombs to fall really near at hand came whistling down and exploded. Everyone stood up and for a moment I think we all felt rather like Brer Rabbit, wondering "what minute was going to be the last". Curiously enough, these first bombs were the nearest so far to EP, so perhaps, as we were then entirely inexperienced in judging bomb distances, there was some excuse for our consternation. Reports of the locations at which the bombs had dropped came through remarkably quickly from Westminster ARP control. All through, the service rendered by the ARP control centres and personnel in giving information of this kind has been first rate. We must take our hats off to the wardens, whose duty it is to locate bombs immediately after they have fallen.

Then we got a report from Ashley Court that power was off and lights low, and later that lights were out. We got out our maps and checking the bomb positions against our mains were able to get a rough idea of what the damage was likely to have been. We had had instructions not to leave shelter unless a serious emergency arose and the present occasion did not call for a sortie.

At 01.30 I rashly decided to try and get some sleep and descended to my camp bed in the cable chase under the 6.6kv switchgear, which had been recommended to me as a safe place. I noticed, however, that the EP resident engineers had staked a claim still lower down in the disused flues of the old boiler house, this being as far down in the bowels of the earth at EP as it was possible to go. Just as I was hanging up my coat the lights gave a sickening lurch and stayed down at about half pressure. I heard a despairing squeal from the rotary in the machine room. I went up on the board and found that the London Power Company voltage had dropped badly. The machine running came off line and our emergency lighting went over automatically to the battery. The general lighting off the A.C. supply was still burning at half pressure. Later, it rose to higher than normal, then fell again, and finally went out altogether. The Power Company's supply had failed, and at EP at any rate we were right out. We stood by until the Power Company came back in about five minutes – good work in view of the nature of the damage to their system which was afterwards reported. All our stations, except those in the Charing Cross district, had been similarly affected, but they all got their moving plant away again very smartly, and the AC supplies came up automatically as soon as the Power Company came back. All station staffs handled this their first serious war emergency, very smartly.'

from Contact *(the CLE Staff Journal), September 1940*

Agnew, a self-styled 'bloody Bevin Boy', described in *Bevin Boy* (1947) what he got out of his encounter with miners, 'a profitable one for both of us':

> We, on our side, learnt a new language – some of it rather bad… But we also learnt the real meaning of several words in our own language. 'Sweat', says the dictionary, is 'moisture from the skin'. For us it is a lot more. It's a memory, a lasting picture, of half-naked bodies, bending, crawling, rolling, heaving, straining to produce that without which we cannot exist. So, too, it is with toil, labour, tears… They mean something idealistic. They represent another world. A world where men fight for their very existence. Where the true meaning of comradeship is appreciated – and practised.

Concentration on the work of men in the pits in wartime can overshadow studies of men and women working in gas and electricity, but some of the latter recorded their memories too (*see left*). 'Remember when no night passed without a raid?' 'L H W', a worker with Central London Electricity, asked in 1941. 'Every flicker of lights made us fear the worst.' Yet on only two occasions had the majority of their customers been unable 'to toast their toes before their bedroom electric fires and cook their breakfast on their electric cookers'. For electricity and gas workers there was a symbolic ending to the war, 'The lights went on again'. A popular song added, comprehensively, 'all over the world'.

Below The Ministry of Information prepared a travelling exhibition for the Ministry of Fuel and Power, to tour the factories in an industrial fuel economy campaign. 'Fuel is Power' was just one of the exhibits.

5

ON THE MOVE

THERE WERE PARTICULAR TIMES during the war when everything seemed to be on the move except those people who were told to stay put. 'Transport went to war' meant transport of materials as much as of troops. On the 180,000 miles of road (as yet there were no motorways), the 20,000 miles of railway track and the 2,000 miles of canal, which scarcely constituted a system or even a 'network', transport was 'in action'. As an official Ministry of War Transport booklet of 1942 put it long before the excitement of D-Day:

> To the fighting man transport is not, indeed, the fighting arm and fist, but it is the blood circulating from the body into that fighting arm and fist. And if bringing down coal from Newcastle or sending the trucks of red ore through the Yorkshire junctions is not as exciting as a dog fight, there is something grave and momentous about this life-blood pumping more rapidly from the heart through the arteries and veins, as this country squares up to fight its enemies.

Heart, blood, arteries, circulation! William Harvey, who discovered circulation of the blood, could have put it no better.

This was the 'Body Politic' at war, and from May 1941, when the Ministry of Transport was merged with the Ministry of Shipping to form a new Ministry of War Transport, Frederick Leathers, raised to the peerage as Woolton had been, was its representative. He had been head of the P&O shipping line and had also been a director of companies involved in coal bunkering. It was not Leathers, however, but Lord Portal, Minister of Works and Buildings, who proclaimed in 1942 that 'the war will be won by that side which can ultimately bring to bear the greatest transport resources and use them efficiently.'

Less has been written about railway workers than about railway directors and railway managers. The fact that the railways had been subjected to national control (with a subsidy in return) has received more attention than the statistics of employment. At one period during the war Britain's railways, along with London Transport, employed nearly 20,000 of their staff not on moving around goods or people, but on the production of armaments, including aircraft, tanks and landing craft, in 35 of their workshops. As early as 1937, two years before the war began, the War

The Railways During Wartime

'Of paramount strategic importance, the British railways, like the Royal Navy, must be somewhat of a "silent service" in wartime. And, without full knowledge of the facts, the public cannot be expected to appreciate how detrimental to the well-being of the railway industry as a whole has been the veil of secrecy under which for security and other reasons, so many of its wartime problems and achievements have been shrouded during the past five years. For with the railway industry, as with most other public services, the goodwill of its users is a sine qua non *for its prosperity.'*

from It Can Now be Revealed *(1947)*

Office had asked the London, Midland and Scottish Railway to design a tank to be produced in its huge works at Crewe, the junction through which much war transport was to pass. Among the tanks eventually built were Covenanters (a name taken from Scottish history), Cruisers, Matildas and Centaurs. Parts were also supplied for Crusaders, Cromwells and Churchills.

It Can Now be Revealed, (*see* left) a booklet compiled in 1945 by the railway companies themselves and issued by the British Railways Press Office, and not by the Ministry of Information, included more photographs of equipment than of workers. There was only one reference *en passant* to women's work. The photographs showed guns, tanks and armoured vehicles along with rafts for battleships and midget submarine superstructures. Particular factories were singled out, such as Swindon, another great railway works, where the first 2,000- and 4,000-pounder bombs were manufactured, the two-thousanders always being referred to as Goebbels and the four-thousanders as Goerings. The booklet also pointed out that a 1,000-bomber strike needed 650 tank cans of petrol.

It was because all such munitions had to be carried by ship and rail that Portal was proved right about transport when he addressed both railwaymen and the public. Generals, who were to play an important part in the history of post-war British Rail, were quick to acknowledge this, particularly after D-Day (6 June 1944), which demanded the biggest of all wartime moves. While preparations were being made for it,

Above Aeroplanes might have to be moved by road, such as these US Mustangs in Spring, 1944: all forms of transport were interconnected. Parts of planes were made in the most unlikely places, including old cotton mills, before being assembled.

Montgomery, in conditions of complete secrecy, addressed 'a representative gathering of railwaymen' of all grades (railwaymen had always been graded) at Euston Station on the afternoon of 22 February, explaining just what needed to be done. Secrecy was maintained as preparatory operations proceeded. They included the building at one station of 17 new marshalling yards and a shed of over 1,000ft in length, complete with overhead electric cranes. During the three weeks preceding 6 June, some 9,700 special trains were run, 3,600 of them in one week, their precious cargoes concealed under tarpaulin sheets. The locomotive drivers and guards who carried them were not photographed. Nor were the goods, the signalmen who controlled the lines, or the stationmasters who waved them through the stations.

Long before D-Day there had been a reversal of railway priorities. Before the war passengers, not yet referred to as customers, came first, in principle at least. The author of *Transport Goes to War* applied the adjective 'sacred' to them, adding that during the war they lost their halo. 'Deliver the passengers, yes; deliver the workers and the

USE SHANKS' PONY

WALK
when you can

AND EASE THE BURDEN WHICH
WAR PUTS ON TRANSPORT

LADIES'
AND
GENTLEMEN'S
HAIRDRESSING
SALOONS
NOW OPEN

Right Less well known than the 'Is Your Journey Really Necessary?' poster at the beginning of this chapter, 'Shanks' Pony' nonetheless conveys the same message more positively. There was far more walking in wartime than there was to be in the 1960s or 1990s.

troops of course [note the order]; but above all deliver the goods. That is what September 1939 meant to British transport.' As for many passengers, they were given exactly the opposite guidance from that set out in pre-war posters. They were now asked the question 'Is your journey really necessary?'

The first people 'on the move' during the war were children, the evacuees of September 1939, many of whom returned home within a few months of transfer and well before the Battle of Britain began. These were often their first journeys by rail. One photograph showed them being carried in a London Transport bus, on the side of which the message 'Goodbye Hitler' had been chalked, perhaps by the children themselves. Such photographs can be compared with those showing the return of the troops from Dunkirk. Throughout 1940, railwaymen and, even more, bus drivers and conductors learned how to operate in the Blitz: 'they worked all night to the tune of the shrapnel'. Sadly there were few photographs of them at work.

By the end of 1941 over 5,000 women were employed on the Southern Railway alone, working as cleaners, porters, booking clerks and ticket collectors; and on the trolley buses in Brighton 44 women conductors set up a national record for regular attendance at work. Absenteeism was less than one per cent.

Trains, particularly expresses, had been a favourite topic for poets and film makers during the 1930s, when there had been seasonal 'Rabbit', 'Broccoli' and

'Strawberry Specials'. In 1942, there were 'coal specials', initially 27 of them a week, then as many as 450:

> You see them coming up the main line as you stand above the scene in the control tower of a great marshalling yard… on all the lines from Crewe or Ashford to the Cardiff yards. Coal has given the railway companies something to think about in the first three years of the War. You will never get a railwayman to believe that coal is short.

Coal figured prominently in the railwayman's imagination as well as in his work. In railway hostels, close to the sidings, sometimes with a 'new set of porcelain baths', there might or might not be central heating. Perhaps it was better if there were not, 'for the one thing that a railwayman admires and sees he gets is an enormous banked up fire. It's very different from the dying clinker of the general waiting room: they do themselves well.' This was voice not of a railwayman, but of a journalist, yet he went on to quote the authentic language of railwaymen of a different grade at work in the railway control rooms:

> For eight hours a day the men who work in the controls do not stop talking. One of them, whistling a dance tune, says 'Hullo, Les, you can turn him out the main now after the express. 2216 is a re-engine for the yard.' 'OK kid, I'll have him turned out. I'll let 614890 go straight?' The whistling goes off. There is a clatter on the line. A sort of moan of glum hopeless anger comes down the wire. A broad and doleful Yorkshire voice says 'Eeh! Hullo! Eeh! I'm 4486. I'm the driver. I've been boompered crawling from signal to signal all morning.'

Below Women were employed in wartime in roughly the same numbers as railwaymen who left to join the Forces: 100,000 of them by 1943.

Right Women were not
spared hard or dirty work.
Here two workers shovel
coal dust on to a truck in a
London railway siding.

Right Women were not
spared hard or dirty work.
Here two workers shovel
coal dust on to a truck in a
London railway siding.

Below 'Carrying on' was
a more reassuring slogan
than 'carrying you'; troop
and freight trains always
had priority. Carriages and
corridors were crowded
and the blackout was
rigorous.

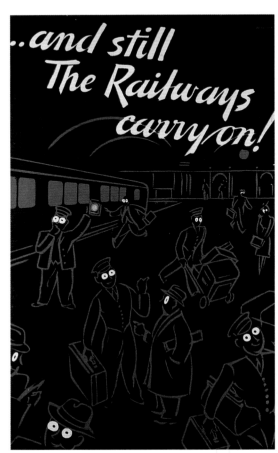

After having been kept waiting for three hours, he is told
that he can go home. 'Hullo kid. There's no hope from that
driver. Loose him off and send him home. Let 4486 come
home late.' For the journalist reporting this conversation,
it was like 'listening to an opera'. The words 'soap opera' had
not yet entered the language.

The Control Room was a male preserve. In the station,
women were at work on the platforms as well as in the
ticket offices. So, indeed, were they in some signal boxes
and in some marshalling yards. A number of them
described their experiences in the railway companies'
magazines (*see* right).

There were 'war heroes' among transport workers in the
days both of the Blitz and of the V1s and V2s. While much
of their work was routine, they had to carry it out in almost
impossible circumstances. A leading shunter, H Davies,
working in a Great Western marshalling yard in London,
wrote an article called 'We Carry On' in which he
described a number of dangerous incidents that had
occurred in black-out conditions. This was one article of
many. There were few parallel articles about signalling.

There were heroines as well as heroes. Thus, Hilda
Reidling, who had been bombed out of her house, joined

the London and North Eastern Railway first as 'porteress' then as a 'motor driver' (a 300 hundredweight Morris lorry) at Maldon East. Her work was tough and brought her into contact with tough people she would never otherwise have met. There was what she called 'one very important matter' which she always bore in mind – 'how to avoid accident'. Reidling was an accomplished dancer, singer and impersonator, and did 'great work' for the Wings of Victory Weeks in Maldon.

Heroines or not, the women were often disposed of quickly by the railways when the war ended. 'Thank You, Ladies, and Goodbye' was the title of a farewell in the magazine of the London and North Eastern Railways showing a group of women workers at the company's wagon works in York. 'Their many-hued overalls and head scarves, their lively chatter in the canteen and their happy gift of repartee will be missed.' 'Your work has been appreciated by the company', it added, but surely the crucial word in this tribute was 'Goodbye'.

Above Female employees at the London North Eastern Railway pictured in November, 1945, in the LNER magazine under the headline 'Thank You, Ladies, and Goodbye'.

My Day's Work

By Miss A G Elsworth, Announcer, York Station

'I always wished to have some job of work that was out of the ordinary, and quite unexpectedly a chance of achieving this ambition was offered to me. The question of introducing lady announcers at York Station was being reviewed and I, along with several other applicants, was given a test – in fact I was "on the air" for the first time in my life. I was lucky enough to be appointed as an Announcer at the Station, where there are now three of us working three different shifts.

My day commences at 8am if it is my turn to take the first shift. I arrive on duty, go into my 'cubby hole', which is situated in such a position as to enable me to see what is happening in the station, switch on the apparatus and set the loud speakers for the requisite platforms. I then talk to members of the public and endeavour to assist them by telling them how to get to their destinations.

Perhaps the most unusual aspect of my new work is the fact that when it falls to my lot to come on duty in the afternoon and work until 10pm I find myself working under "black-out" conditions. It is certainly strange to have to announce the arrival of trains which one can scarcely see, but to help me to overcome this difficulty I can watch the automatic indicator which tells me which platforms are occupied. On several occasions when a "purple" warning has been received I have had to work by the light of a handlamp and rely on the signalmen and the indicator to know when the trains are arriving. When the "red" warning is received I have to inform the members of the public that they may travel if they wish to do so as trains continue to run as usual and the work goes on as if nothing out of the ordinary has taken place, often to the accompaniment of the drone of enemy planes overhead – it is all part of one's day's work.'

from the **London & North Eastern Railway Magazine**

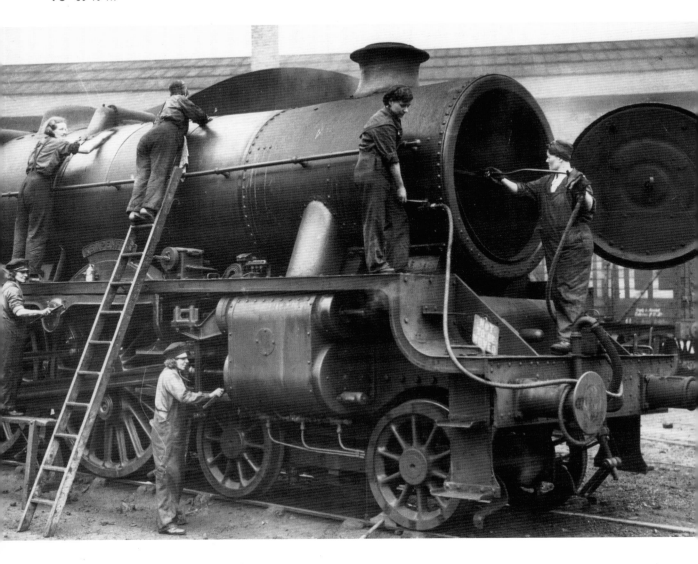

Above These women were employed as engine cleaners at a north London depot. It was the first time that they had been given access to locomotives.

Far right, top Mrs and Miss March (the latter pictured here), and their boat *Heather Bell*, played 'an earnest and useful part in the war effort'.

Another company, the Great Western Railway, was still showing on the front page of its magazine a photograph of a woman worker in January 1946. She was one of 16,000 women still 'carrying on' in the company. The GWR made a film *Women at War* (1945): one still shows a woman replacing the lamp on a signal high above the line; another has engine cleaners in a busy shed. No film, however, a company spokesman observed, could 'do more than faint justice to the scope and variety of the tasks undertaken by GWR women; nor can any picture give an idea of the training in technicalities which was the necessary prelude to the tackling of the job.'

Women were prominent, too, as volunteers on the canals on which traffic had been low before the War. During the war 12 million tons of supplies were carried by canal each year. A Ministry of Information photograph, entitled 'Women Run a Boat', showed Mrs and Miss March of Worcester in their boat *Heather Bell*, which regularly made the journey from Worcester through the Midlands with a variety of cargoes, including coal (*see* right).

The press and the public were highly sympathetic towards the boatmen, their wives and children, although the nature of their work meant that they were not a group with whom the press or public were in frequent contact. Those who worked on the railways and bus crews were, with transport to and from work a burden for the passengers. Travelling, and the attendant difficulties, would become a 'vivid part' of the memory of their war experience (*see* below).

It is interesting to compare memories such as this with one unusually sharp comment in *The War Illustrated* in July 1941 accompanying a photograph of the crowded car park at Epsom on Derby Day. 'Ponder well the top photograph', the writer of the article told his readers. 'The owners of all these cars have used precious petrol to go to the Derby.' He chose as his title, 'Yes, They "Went to It" – the Derby – with a Will'.

An Aycliffe Memory

"'A vast network of trains and buses ferried people to and from the factory… Buses had to be highly organised to fit shift times and pick up along complicated routes. That travelling is a very vivid part of the memory: it could be pretty frightening walking to a stop or station in thick black-out darkness.

"We went up steps, a load of steps, across a bridge, down the steps to the other side, and every morning the girls used to have the carriage doors open pulling me in as the train was moving."

"You were always late, were you?"

"Always late, always late for everything. I was late for my own wedding – yes. Not through my own fault but funnily enough I was late for my own wedding. After the war, after it was all over, I met girls that I'd worked with and they used to laugh about that you know – they pulled me into the train every time. They used to be all yelling out of the windows 'hurry up', and me mother used to say 'you'll be late – one of the these days you'll have a heart attack running like you do'. I used to get up on a morning at half past four and it was pitch black as you know, there was no lights anywhere, and I used to get my sister up (she was always asleep). I was always the one who was more alert than Iris (that's my sister). And she'd come downstairs and we would just have a cup of tea; and I always liked my cigarettes ('Fag Ash Lil'). Iris didn't smoke, but I smoked – it used to be a cigarette and a cup of tea – Iris used to have a sandwich, or a bit of toast or something, and then I just used to put the haversack on her (and she'd still be asleep) put a scarf round her head, and I put my scarf on. We all wore trousers of course, and she used to tuck her arm in mine and we used to walk out the house to the bus stop at Norton – wait till the bus came up, got on the bus (Iris still asleep) – walk up Bishopton Lane, at Stockton, to the station for five minutes to six, and the train would come from Middlesbrough… then it would come to South Bank and then Middlesbrough, picking us all up, and picked us up at Stockton station. Then we would get out at Aycliffe (Iris still asleep) – before we got into Aycliffe I used to wake Iris up and she used to take her hairpins out and stand and try to comb her hair and make herself a bit respectable.'"

from A Pamphlet to Commemorate the First Reunion of the
Women who Worked in Aycliffe Munitions Factory 1940–1945 *(1989)*

6

STITCHES IN TIME

"MAKE-DO AND MEND!' could be as comprehensive a slogan as 'Dig, Dig, Dig!', and both the making-do and the mending covered far more activities than those carried out in the textile industries, which had been in decline in the 1930s and which do not feature at all in the index of Calder's *The People's War*. Clothes do, however, and fashion, and so also – introducing a new wartime name – do 'utility goods'. These covered furniture, as well as dresses and suits, both rationed; but it was the clothes that were most discussed in the press.

The title of this chapter makes it clear that it does not cover furniture, but it incorporates war work on other items as different as barrage balloons and boots and shoes, and it gives a time dimension to the advice. This was always related to circumstances more than to principles. Stitches in time might save lives, as well as 'points': in days of rationing you could choose within your clothing points ration what items to buy. The slogan had a practical point too. 'A stitch in time not only saves extra work in the end, but precious coupons.'

After 1942, the chief minister in the background of the branches of war production covered in this chapter was Hugh Dalton, President of the Board of Trade, who had hitherto been in charge of economic warfare. On taking office in 1942, he was warned by the Archbishop of Canterbury that the Church was suffering from the reduction in the number of people working in the textile industries and from controls placed on their output: 'a grave shortage of hassocks was likely'.

There were more possibilities in this jeopardised sphere of mobilising voluntary effort, much of it carried out in the home, than there were in many others, and in other

Right A London County Council Make-do and Mend class stand at a domestic front exhibition in 1943. On show are renovated dresses and children's garments and toys, all made out of old clothes.

Left There was more to textiles than spindles and looms. In this general view of a carbonising shed a worker (on the right) is feeding the shaker that removes the carbon dust from rags. The worker on the left is packing shaken rags into a sheet for delivery to the 'shoddy' works. In the background the acid container of the carbonising plant is being charged with liquid hydrochloric acid. The chemical industry flourished in wartime with a diminished labour force. The huge chemicals concern, Imperial Chemical Industries (ICI), was fully employed, though not in lines that would have been its own peacetime priorities.

kinds of stitching there was also ample scope for voluntary effort. Indeed, it was at the core of much of the work discussed. When clothes rationing was introduced in 1941 Lyttelton was President of the Board of Trade. The rationing, announced in a broadcast by Lyttelton, allowed adults only around half their pre-war 'consumption of clothing', with everything depending, of course, on the size and quality of their pre-war wardrobes. 'Make-do and Mend' was often necessary, not just advisable. Some official early advice was gratuitous:

> In the War we must learn as civilians to be seen in clothes that are not so smart... because we are bearing yet another share in the War. When you feel tired of your old clothes, remember that by making them do, you are contributing to some part of an aeroplane, a gun or a tank.

Other advice was more acceptable, particularly for women: 'No material must lie idle – so be a magician and turn all old clothes into new'.

In Wartime

production must be for war and not for peace. Here are examples of the changeover from peacetime products to wartime necessities:

CORSETS *become* Parachutes and Chinstraps
LACE CURTAINS *become* Sand-fly Netting
CARPETS *become* Webbing Equipment
TOILET PREPARATIONS *become* Anti-Gas Ointments
GOLF BALLS *become* Gas Masks
MATTRESSES *become* Life Jackets
SAUCEPANS *become* Steel Helmets
COMBS *become* Eyeshields

Issued by The Board of Trade

Making barrage balloons, parachutes and tents was a very necessary task in 1939 and 1940. One factory that made parachutes employed women who, before the war, had made everything from corsets to handbags. They were supervised by Mrs Doris Wilkinson, who emphasised later in the war that the factory 'had never had a failure'. She had passed out 'tens of thousands of parachutes, and that meant inspecting millions and millions of yards of stitching'.

Barrage-balloon makers were often photographed. So, too, were women making airmen's flying suits. The barrage-balloon makers were described as 'crawling through silver-grey landscapes of endless cotton and synthetic rubber'. 'A balloon starts like a jumble sale where everyone is trying to buy a patch', one caption to a photograph read.

Less publicity was devoted to the people making soldiers' or sailors' uniforms. Yet in May 1941 a *Reynolds News* reporter, Tom Clarke, visited, without providing an accompanying photograph, a big factory in London's East End where 2,000 men, women and girls were turning out uniforms for 'our fighting men on land, at sea and in the air'. Perhaps the reason why there was no photograph was that the part of

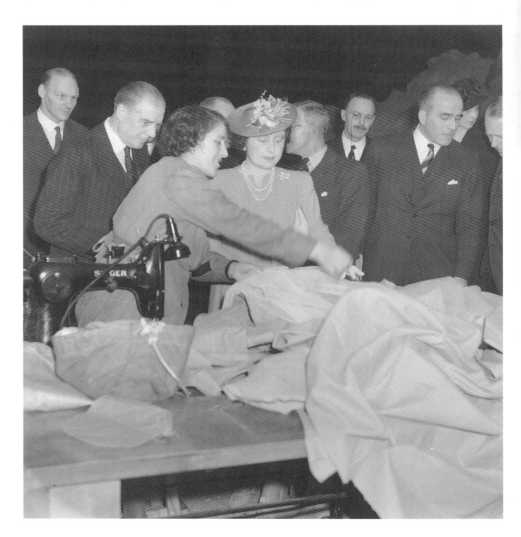

London where the factory was located presented 'a melancholy panorama of destruction', but Clarke had found it a tonic 'to go and see the people carrying on with their jobs and with hearts still singing on' (a difficult operation).

There were 15 different operations in making a battledress, and it improved the rate of 'cutting and stitching' if there was music while the textile workers were making battledress or sailors' trousers. 'If we put the news on over the radio loudspeakers', the Welfare Supervisor told the journalist, 'it stops the work, but put *Tipperary* or some other lively thing on and they go to it like the devil'.

Far away in Lancashire, where Gracie Fields had made her name by singing old and new songs, there was a demand in the middle of the war for cotton workers, and women who had worked in the cotton industry before the war — as always, they were its mainstay — were required to register in September 1943 (*see* p86). There was also increasing demand for workers in woollen textiles across the Pennines. Soon the main effort in clothing was to produce men's suits for returned, demobilised servicemen. Montague Burton's was the main supplier. His employees had contributed half the cost of a Spitfire, and Burton himself the other other half in 1940. It was known as the 'Montague Bee'. By 1943 the periodical *Men's Wear* was coming into its own again.

WOMEN
who have worked in the
COTTON INDUSTRY

WHY you have had to
register today

You have a right to know

BRIEFLY :—The Nation needs the special skill
which only the women who know cotton
have. We need more cotton for the big
bombers and bomber tyres, for parachutes,
tarpaulins, uniforms and a host of war
purposes, and for essential civilian services

No one but an experienced cotton worker
will meet this need, and some of you will,
therefore, have to return to cotton

Today you take your place alongside the
miners, the shipbuilders, the marine engineers
and the nurses who have preceded you in
special registration in order that your skill
may, like theirs, be used where it is most
vitally needed

**THE OUTPUT
OF COTTON GOODS
MUST GO UP NOW**

P.I. 132 1943   September, 1943

Above This highly posed
photograph and the
Sphere caption that
accompanies it take us
to a London suburb:
'Britain is near the end
of the fourth year of war,
yet her women can still
look like the girls in this

picture. This, to a great
extent, is thanks to
Utility clothes, which,
introduced 18 months
ago, have done much
to keep women smart'.
The cyclist is wearing
a design 'appropriately
named Battledress'.

There had been a major change in the clothing industry in 1942 when a selected range of utility clothes made their way into the shops. They included both men's and women's clothes and set a new standard of quality. There were no pleats or trouser turn-ups, but the Utility rules left colour out of the range of control and, to a limited extent, design. The main emphasis at the time of the introduction of the scheme was on price. *Vogue* magazine praised women's Utility clothes, calling them 'beautifully designed', adding pertinently that they were 'suitable to [women's] lives and incomes'.

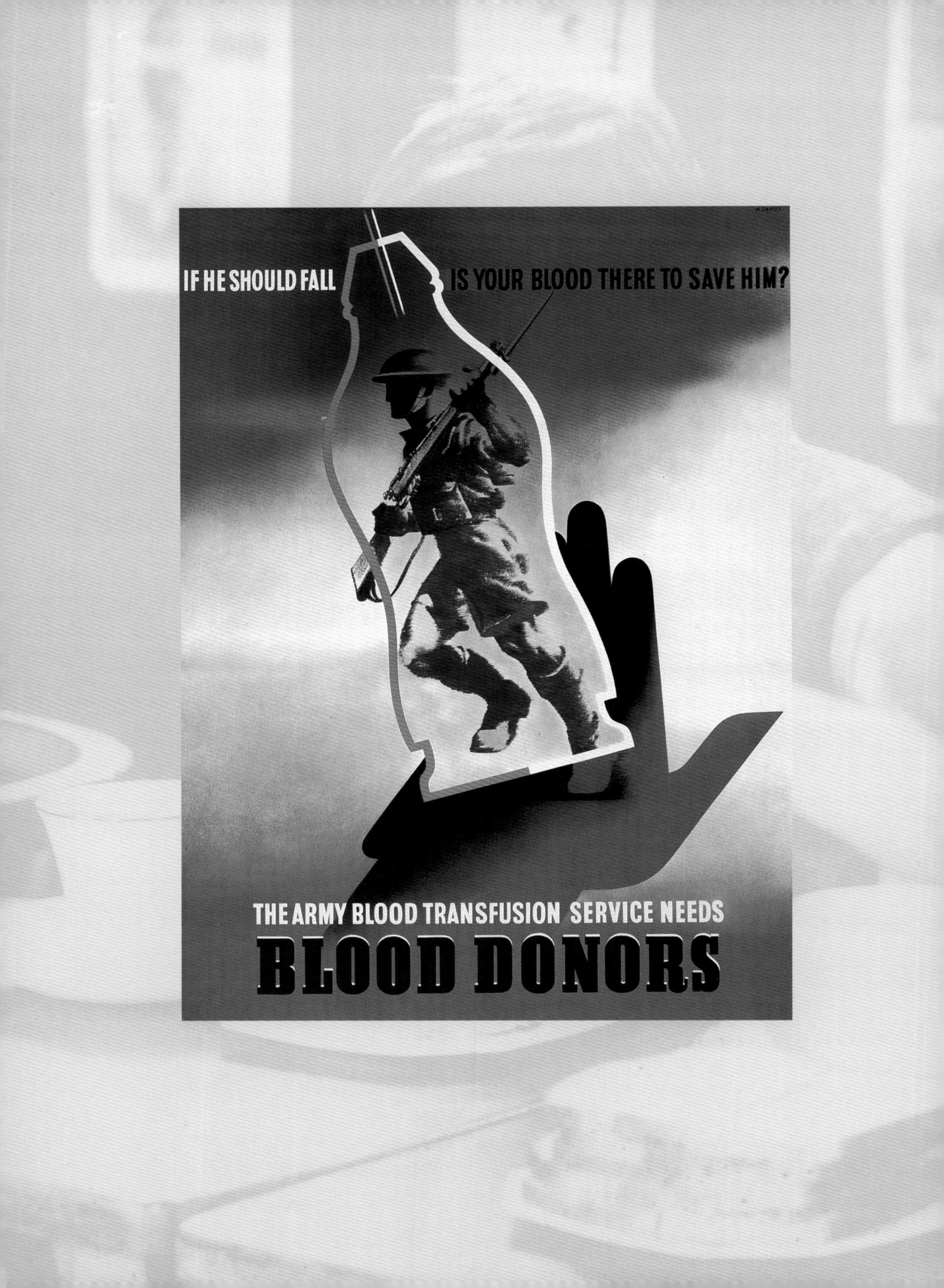
IF HE SHOULD FALL
IS YOUR BLOOD THERE TO SAVE HIM?
THE ARMY BLOOD TRANSFUSION SERVICE NEEDS
BLOOD DONORS

7

HEALTH AND WELFARE

I T IS A DEBATABLE POINT as to which should be placed first in the title of this chapter: health or welfare. A war regarded as a 'people's war' required more than welfare slogans. Policies leading up to legislative measures had to figure on the agenda and, after the war, such legislation was to culminate in a 'welfare state', a term little used during the war itself. Meanwhile, as long as the war lasted there were measurable improvements in health, owing more to diet (and the elimination of unemployment) than to medical art and science. Infant mortality fell. So too did the incidences of tuberculosis, one of a number of 'mass killer' diseases at the outbreak of war.

After the end of the war a heralded National Health Service was begun, thought by its creators to be at the very heart of the welfare state. It had its origins in the wartime Emergency Hospitals Service and a series of behind-the-scenes discussions involving doctors, ministers and civil servants. Meanwhile, an improved blood transfusion service was a physical link between workers and fighters.

In one of the most influential of Sir Keith Hancock's official war histories, that on *Social Policy*, written by Richard Titmuss, it was pointed out that 1940, the year of Dunkirk, the year of greatest danger during the war when Britain stood alone, was also the year of a great historical turn. Reforms were introduced then that had been

Below This photograph, entitled 'New War Opens on a Factory Front', shows the Medical Research Council, on behalf of the Ministry of Health, carrying out a radiography survey for tuberculosis. *Picture Post* produced many excellent photographs, including one emphasising that tuberculosis was no longer one of the 'tragic incurable diseases. Medical science can beat it'. Four hundred people a day might line up to be X-rayed.

Left As these 'Lend Lease children' eat, they are reminded of where their eggs came from. One of the main Lend Lease aids was dried eggs; another, leaving lasting memories, was tinned spam. The Poultry Association objected to the former, but lost.

deemed impossible during the 1930s, reforms that were directly to affect the post-war generation. Expectant and nursing mothers received a guaranteed ration of milk: a pint a day. The use of milk in the manufacture of chocolates and in ice-cream was prohibited. Home-produced fruit juice was offered, soon to be augmented with Lend Lease orange juice as part of a vitamin supplementation scheme.

In such implementations of policy it was difficult to separate welfare and health. Nor was it made easier when the study and practice of occupational medicine was given a great boost during the War, linking the factory with the laboratory. There was

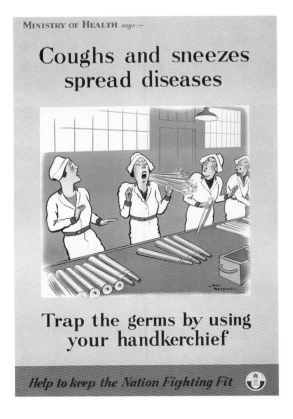

still no revolution in antibiotics, but the successful wartime application of what quickly became the best-known of them, penicillin, was described by Walter Elliot, a former Conservative Minister of Health, as the best news of 1943, better even than the news of Stalingrad. Penicillin was not available, however, to the civilian population.

Some wartime articles dealt with health, including one interesting article in January 1945 by Charles Graves in *The Sphere*, to which he gave the title 'Your Very Good Health'. Graves noted the fall of infant mortality rates in 1943 to an 'all-time low record' and the decline in typhoid fever and diphtheria, but he added that 'there can be little doubt that the minor ills of the population' had increased. Fortunately, however, as far as 'the nerves of the nation' were concerned, 'attendances at mind-treatment clinics' were 'below the pre-war level, and so [were] the admissions to mental hospitals'. While admitting that factory workers had been extremely well treated by the Ministry of Food (Graves rightly devoted more attention to that ministry than the Ministry of Health), and that their health services and canteen meals were 'admirable' (an exaggeration), 'the unfortunate civilians not engaged in war work' (a curious way of putting it) 'must feel irritated to be told by the Ministry that their health has improved'.

Graves's general conclusion, as his title suggested, was that 'the health of the country is surprisingly good. The necessity for eating more green vegetables to supplement the exiguous meat ration has had a very good effect on the population. The extra walking compelled by lack of transport has also been beneficial.' He had one regret – that 'yoghurt, the specially treated buttermilk, which balances diets so well, cannot be bought all over the country'. There were other commentators who directed attention to the increased wartime interest in collecting plants for medicinal use. A 1942 article in *Women's Institute News*, for example, gave instructions for collecting green dormant shoots of broom (*Cytisus scoparius*) in springtime. The drug that they contained, sparteine, was being employed in the treatment of high blood pressure.

Graves did not mention hospitals. Yet they figured prominently in wartime, particularly when civilians were injured in bomber raids and when wounded soldiers were brought back home. They might have figured even more prominently, of course, had the country been immediately subjected to the kind of air attack envisaged before 1939. There are photographs of hospital surgeons at work in what

Below Edward Ardizzone: *A Basement Ward at the Royal Herbert Hospital Woolwich (c1941).*

were often cramped conditions, and some interesting paintings of hospital interiors by war artists. There were also campaigns to recruit nurses, some of whom had moved out of nursing into other kinds of war work. The profession, not well paid, was already experienced recruiting problems that were to loom large after the war, and that were only partially solved by employment of nurses from the Commonwealth.

There were more nurses in factories than there were in doctors' surgeries; and welfare within the factory began with precautions against accidents, the consequences of which nurses, including volunteers, would have to handle. Some of the precautions were obvious, like guard systems around machines or covering hair to prevent it getting entangled in machines. One poster read 'Gearwheels Catch Cloth. Keep Your Guard On'. Another, produced in co-operation with the Royal Society for the Prevention of Accidents, simply showed a ladder suggesting that it would be wise to examine it before use. 'Broken Rungs Cause Broken Limbs'. Whether the posters changed practices cannot be proved, but their direct appeal to the immediate interest of the war worker – with no cross references to morale or to the war effort – suggests that they did.

Some company histories dealing with the war years (like that of Ford, *see* p118) explained that, under the overall supervision of a War Safety Committee, the accident rate for the years 1940 to 1944 inclusive was less than that in 1939. The committee met once a month, reviewed the accidents that had taken place, discussed their causes and their remedies, and was 'tireless in preaching the two virtues: cleanliness and tidiness'.

The Chorley Royal Ordnance Factory, which offered its workers a free supply of protective creams and special soap, had its own laundry that washed 10,000 protective garments and 142,000 hand towels each week. It also repaired an average of 400 pairs of 'Danger Area' shoes.

Factory welfare was concerned with more than safety, however, particularly as far as women war workers were concerned. *Fabian Quarterly*, a Labour publication, devoted an article to it by Mary Sur in July 1945, summarising 'wartime developments'. Everything had 'hung fire' during the 'phoney war', Sur recalled, but with the arrival of Bevin, the word 'welfare' began to appear in many official documents. The Ministry of Labour appointed Outside Welfare Officers to handle the problems of transferred workers; the Factories (Medical and Welfare) Order gave the Chief Inspector of Factories power to insist upon the appointment of doctors, nurses or welfare officers in

Far left, above and below
Three posters reflecting the government's concern over nursing staffing levels and the link between productivity and accidents at work.

Above Another poster
warning of the dangers at
work makes explicit the
link with productivity.

Below Accidents did
happen of course.
This is the clinic in a
Royal Ordnance factory.

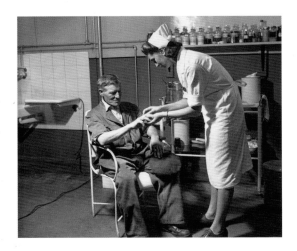

any factory engaged in carrying out war work that he
deemed to be necessary.

Soon there was a spontaneous demand from below,
encouraged by the shop stewards' movement, whose
activities worried Bevin as much as they did Churchill.
Nevertheless, Bevin went on to press for the development
of war production committees with the support of other
ministers, particularly Cripps. The number of welfare and
personnel officers in factories increased from about 1,500
in 1939 to 5,500 in 1945.

The same broadening of welfare objectives was apparent
in the case of miners as well. In its White Paper of 1942
(*see* page 64) the government set out its intention to
establish a Medical Consultative Service for the mines.
Before the war one man in five among underground
workers in coal mines received compensation for accident
or disease and, despite all the difficulties of maintaining
the mines in wartime, the position did not deteriorate.
There were, indeed, other war industries with a worse
record of accidents.

Absenteeism, of great interest to Mass Observation, was
a different matter. It was also of great interest to the
Industrial Health Research Board of the Medical Research Council, which produced
an official report on the subject in 1943. Most of the women studied were said to be
satisfied with their jobs and with most of the working conditions: the biggest 'worry'
– and worry led to absenteeism – was connected with men overseas, husbands or
sweethearts. Health came second and home life third.

The Welfare Officer at the Risley Royal Ordnance Factory, C McIntyre,
concentrated properly on the factory itself. She wrote a note on absenteeism, sadly
undated, which is in the archives of the Imperial War
Museum. 'The working day [a tough twelve hour day]... is
a very big problem', she believed. So was the travel time
added on to it, particularly for women who, before joining
the factory, had been employed in domestic service.
Motivations were low and there was a stultifying 'rivalry'
between workers in the 'clean areas' and the rest.

McIntyre rightly considered that any improvement had to
go beyond the clean towels and regular supplies of fresh
soap that she herself had recommended. 'If we treat the
workers with respect, then the workers will give the factory
some respect too.' Outside her remit, she argued that
financial incentives were necessary. 'If the employees reach

a target for production, then they should be given an increase in their salary [sic] or a Sunday morning off.'

It is not surprising that intelligent and highly motivated observers from outside should advise workers that 'the Welfare Worker is completely and utterly on your side'. As Grace Herbert, who travelled from Fleet Street to 'a munitions town', put it in 1941, 'these days she [the Welfare Worker] is young and attractive, much more liable than the old type to get her way with the boss'. One of them had told her that 'for the Welfare Worker wisdom comes from the heart' to which Herbert had replied, 'and a sense of humour too'. She had in mind not only bosses, but foremen, who played a big role in most factories. She was writing too generally. Personal reminiscences do not fully corroborate her story.

When a journalist, Norman Robson, asked the question in the same year 'Welfare in Factories: Fad or Necessity?' he had no doubt about the answer. It was neither a fad nor a whim of Bevin. Ensuring the 'welfare of our Wartime Working Millions' was a necessity, and he quoted as evidence the words of an industrialist – 'If the workers at home are discontented, it does not matter what the armies do in the field'. That might have been going too far, but Robson was surely right to conclude that 'welfare facilities in industry have come to stay as an essential part of industrial life'.

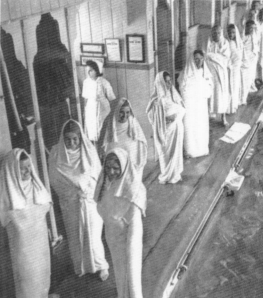

Above Looking like Egyptian mummies, war workers on rest cure take the brine bath at Droitwich Spa.

Rest Breaks in the Country for Overworked War Workers

'Breakfast in bed is one of the pleasures during the first few days of their stay in the rest-break house in Tadworth to which war workers from London and the south of England go for a well-earned rest.

These rest-break houses are something new in our industrial system. Holiday hostels and convalescent homes have always existed, but the object of the rest-break homes is to revive the flagging worker before she becomes ill from overwork or worry arising out of war conditions.

Everything is done to make the rest, usually a fortnight, a complete change. The ideal house accommodates not more than fifty girls and seldom as many. There were thirty-four girls at Tadworth the day I went there. The house is not run on institutional lines – there is only one rule: in bed by 10.30. Once a week, when there is a dance in the village, the rule is relaxed; but the girls are very willing to keep to the rule on six nights of the week.

The times of meals, too, are fixed to suit girls on holiday. Breakfast at nine-thirty; dinner at one, and a high tea at five forty-five, leaving a long afternoon for walking or visiting the many beauty spots nearby. Hot drinks and sandwiches are provided at nine-thirty. The rooms are large and airy, the garden not too formal. There are always deck chairs and rugs on the porch so that the girls can just sit about, if that's what they want to do, but walking and shop-gazing are two of the occupations the girls love after their sedentary jobs.

Mrs Ellis, the warden (this is a heavy word for such a charming, informal hostess) told me about the rest-break houses in other parts of the country; she has seen them grow from the very early stages. She and her sister were the first wardens in the first hut that was opened in North Wales.'

from Woman *magazine, summer 1943*

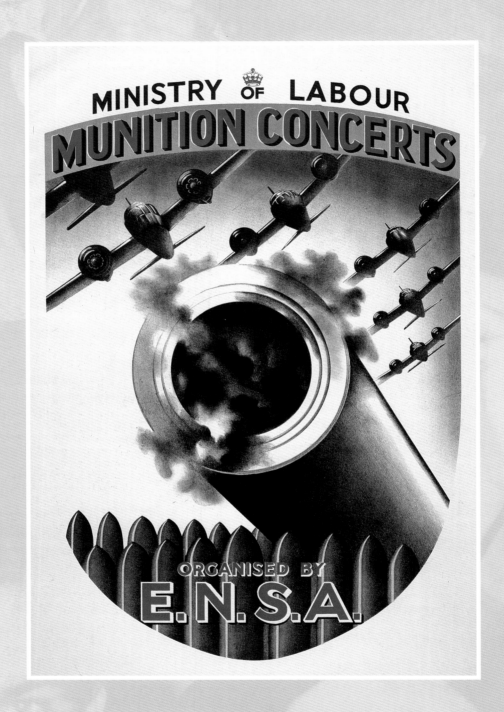

WORKERS' PLAYTIME

WHEN THE WAR STARTED, the periodical *Melody Maker*, widely read 'in the trade' and as good a source for the history of wartime morale as Mass Observation, claimed that music – and it had popular music in mind – was coming 'right into its own'. Its headline ran 'A Jazz Accompaniment to the March of Time'. Apart from Sandy MacPherson playing – it seemed to some incessantly – at the BBC's Theatre Organ, the 'phoney war', despite the jokes, began drearily. The Home Office ruled that 'all cinemas, dance halls and places of public entertainment' were to be 'closed until further notice'. BBC television, then seen only by a tiny well-off London audience, stopped abruptly in the middle of a Mickey Mouse cartoon. Football matches and 'outdoor meetings of all kinds which bring large numbers together' also came to an end.

Controls remained, but most total bans, except that on television, were quickly lifted, and 'entertainers' of all kinds were confident (rightly) that they were making their own distinctive contribution to the war effort. By Christmas 1939 the dance halls were full, and so were the cinemas. One of the first films about the war, *The Lion Has Wings* (1939), opened with the commentator pronouncing solemnly, 'This is England where we believe in democracy'. Many of the best jokes came from Tommy Handley, ensconced in the first *ITMA* programmes ('It's That Man Again') above his Office of Twerps (Mr Fusspot, played by Jack Train, was at his side) in his Ministry of Aggravation and Mysteries. Mr Fusspot's punchline was 'This is most irregular'. One of Handley's first actions was to place Jack Hylton's Band under direct Ministry control.

Further *ITMA* series registered changes on the Home Front. The Ministry of Aggravation and Mysteries was evacuated ('Foaming at the Mouth' was a new location: 'It's That Sand Again'); a newcomer in 1941, Mrs Mopp (Dorothy Summers: 'Can I do you now, Sir?') strained carrot jelly through her jumper; in 1942 'Foaming at the Mouth' welcomed a war factory that Handley managed; and before the war ended it was transformed into a spa, then a hotel.

Music had its place in *ITMA*, as it did in films. It was, as earlier chapters in this book have shown, an accompaniment to the war experience, and through the songs of the

Entertainment and Propaganda

'The injection of propaganda into entertainment programmes with a totally different object… is very seldom, in our experience, successful and results in failure both of the propaganda and of the surrounding programme through the irritation caused in the listener's mind by the feeling he is being got at.'

BBC internal letter, 9 Oct 1942

'Why not make Picture Post a department of the Ministry of Information? You've got a knack with propaganda, not only for foreign readers, but for home consumption, too. After those desert battle pictures, it was a genius to print the village wedding. Somehow, it makes even fighting worth while when you see the precious things you're fighting for.'

letter to Picture Post, 9 March 1942

period a source of future nostalgia. Nor was it only the range of music covered in *Melody Maker* that was heard: the operatic soprano Joan Cross sang, for example, 'The Last Rose of Summer'. Classical music figured in workers' concerts. Thus, at a factory in the north-west in April 1943, Yehudi Menuhin played his violin before no fewer than 6,000 workers and was shown in a photograph surrounded by women anti-aircraft workers. One of them, 22-year-old Dorothy Arkle, secured his autograph on a £1 note: she had nothing else to write on.

Bevin, speaking at a factory concert in July 1940 (in the presence of the comedian Will Fyffe, who performed before Bevin did), put it in his own inimitable way: 'Well mates, I believe that besides saying "Go to It" we should say "Sing With It".' It was a welcome immediately seized upon by the press. Bevin went on to tell the audience about the quartet in the government who would 'work the entertainment scheme':

Above The pianist and conductor Carroll Gibbons, who had made his reputation with the Savoy Orphans and was well-known to a large radio audience, entertains attentive war workers in the spring of 1942. His distinctive, smooth style won him many admirers.

Right Ernie Bevin with his 'honourable mates' in July 1940: the Minister of Labour was as enthusiastic about factory music as any official in the ministry, or, indeed, any worker on the shop floor.

Morrison; Beaverbrook; A V Alexander, First Lord of the Admiralty; and himself. The concert was broadcast by the BBC and attracted great publicity.

Later in the war, Bevin Boys, scarcely his mates, sang songs of which Bevin might not have approved in the setting either of hostels or mines. On his first night in a Bevin Boys' hostel, one uneasy newcomer could not get to sleep because his fellow noviciates, just returned from the pubs, spent an hour in a community singsong: old songs, new songs, sad songs, happy songs, sentimental songs and filthy songs. They had 'an apparently inexhaustible repertoire'.

One of the songs, many of which were 'unrepeatable', was a melancholy ditty sung to the tune of *Paper Doll*:

As I walked down the street the other day,
A damsel turned to me and she did say:
'Why aren't you in khaki or navy blue
And fighting for your country like the other boys do?'
I turned to her and this I did reply
The answer nearly made the poor girl cry!
'The army I have tried to join
But Bevin sent me down the mine
And left me with a broken heart.'

There was ample entertainment presented 'from below' during the war.

Those who were so copiously entertained by 'the authorities' willingly entertained themselves. Many of them preferred to do so. Dancing was much appreciated, and Victor Silvester was as popular on the working front as on the fighting front, where opportunities for actually dancing were more restricted.

Bevin himself had taken the initiative in arranging public entertainment for war workers. In the summer of 1940 he wrote a letter to the Chairman of the Board of Management of the NAAFI, the organisation managing servicemen's canteens, asking for his sympathy and support for a proposal to provide entertainment for munitions workers with the object of stimulating production. Both the NAAFI and the Ministry of Labour, he suggested, could jointly use the resources of ENSA (the Entertainments National Service Association). An active alliance was quickly achieved, and towards the end of July NAAFI/ENSA concerts were being held in factories, the first of them in a London munitions factory that was described as 'somewhere in England'. Soon they were being staged in all parts of England, one at Wolverhampton, for example, another at Sheffield, and in South Wales and Scotland too. They were reported at length in the local press. In the north of England, 'local talent' was used. A woman worker in an aircraft factory, 19-year-old Winifred Dalton, led her fellow workers in song and then, without difficulty, encouraged them to dance. The following day she was to marry a private soldier just back from Dunkirk. The factory managers described the occasion as 'a tonic to the workers – especially to the girls'.

Above This page reproduced from *ENSA Picture News* reveals an 'entertainment drive', itself a model of productivity.

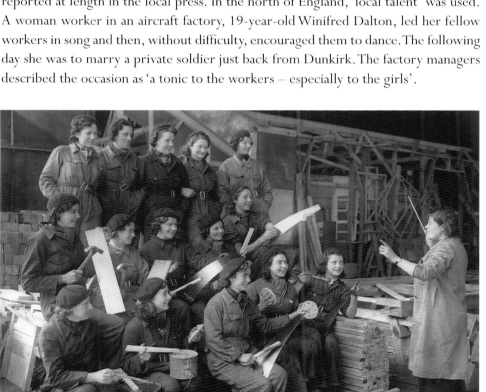

Left The instruments in this 'orchestra' owe much to the factory workers' resourcefulness (although the sound was not recorded). The conductor here, Miss Andrew, supervised women carpenters who were making huts in a south-coast factory .

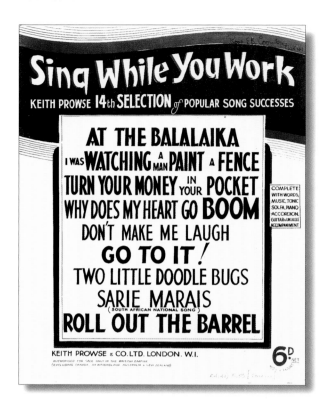

Above Some songs sold well in sheet form during the war – this was before transistor radio– and there were collections of songs old and new. The ticketseller Keith Prowse's 14th selection of 'Popular Song Successes' included a number called 'Go To It!'. Sadly it was not a success and did not survive the war as did Vera Lynn's songs.

ENSA, directed by Basil Dean, became uneasy about the use of non-professional performers and pressed Bevin hard to ensure that the contribution of professionals to the national war effort was fully recognised. It did not refer to them as 'working' while they entertained, but it wanted what it judged to be an adequate proportion of professionals to be treated as though they belonged to a reserved occupation. Meanwhile, in October 1940, the Ministry of Labour and the three Services ministries had set up an inter-departmental Entertainments Board and a 'system' had been devised that was to last throughout the war.

Inevitably, it involved the BBC. The first *Music While You Work* programme had been broadcast before the first of the NAAFI/ENSA concerts (200 factories in 1940: 2,200 in 1944) and it soon became a favourite not only with factory audiences, but also with housewives in their own homes. Its first opening announcement ran 'Go to it. Carry on Workers', but this was changed to 'Calling All Workers'; and after the programme had become highly popular with workers and housewives, as well as with servicemen, the words were changed in 1944 to 'Calling All Forces and Workers'.

The BBC programme picked out in the title of of this chapter, *Workers' Playtime* (*see* p16), was originally scheduled in May 1941 for a six weeks' run. It was so successful that Bevin spoke again across the air when it went into a new series, declaring that 'it makes us all feel that we are working together in the common cause to win the War'. The programme too moved with the times, and towards the end of the war in April 1945, a special *Workers' Playtime* for housewives was broadcast

Workers' Playtime

'I am glad to be able to tell you that from all the Ministry of Labour and National Service's Regional Offices the report is the same, namely, that BBC Workers' Playtime is a most popular form of entertainment. Reports indicate that workers are keen to listen to these broadcasts; that it is looked upon as definitely sustaining morale; and that in some cases increased production has been noted, particularly amongst women. Good technique in presentation is a special feature. Some of the success is due to the fact that well-known artists take part who are to be seen only on rare occasions outside London. The feature gives a sense of kinship with workers elsewhere who are listening to the broadcast.'

letter from the Ministry of Labour and National Service to the BBC, 18 November 1943

from Rugby (the phrase 'somewhere in England' had long since gone). Tickets, issued by the Ministry of Labour, were handed also out through Factory Welfare Departments to workers in various local factories and to the Women's Voluntary Service, which was said by the *Rugby Advertiser* 'to have given considerable assistance in solving war workers' problems'. At the concert members of the WVS acted as door stewards and ushers. The by then well-known compere of the show, Bill Gates, was given a tremendous welcome. He had become a celebrity, like many of the performers whom he introduced.

Less attention has been paid to workers' orchestral concerts than to the famous Myra Hess concerts in the National Gallery, the first of which was held in October 1939 in the days of the 'phoney war'. Yet one given by the BBC Northern Orchestra in November 1943, in the Rolls Royce factory canteen at Crewe, was to be remembered long afterwards. A Special Souvenir programme listed compositions by Schubert, Bach, Mozart and Tchaikovsky (as a Russian, his music was immensely popular in 1943) and ended with Offenbach's *Orpheus in the Underworld*. All the items had been selected from requests forwarded by employees. Beaverbrook's *Daily Express* had seen only 'madness' in the setting up of CEMA ('there is no such thing as culture in war time'), the Council for the Encouragement of Music and the Arts, but by the time Crewe celebrated, Beaverbrook too would no doubt have thrown his hat in the air for Tchaikovsky, if not for Bach. Bevin thought CEMA too highbrow, but in this case not all workers were on his side.

At no point during the war was 'culture' at the centre of discussion. A less acceptable term than 'welfare', it was associated more with 'the enemy' than with 'the allies'. The furthest CEMA could go was to talk of 'cultural services'. Yet out of CEMA the post-war Arts Council was to emerge. Horizons widened, not narrowed, when Britain was cut off from continental Europe, and wise men and women knew that, as the long war continued, there was far more to the process of increasing access to the arts than sustaining morale.

Left One of the ENSA classical concerts, in early 1945, specially planned for war workers. The initials CEMA (Council for the Encouragement of Music and the Arts) were less well known than ENSA by war workers.

THE YOUNG AND THE OLD

ENERATIONAL DIFFERENCES both in attitudes to work and in social behaviour were noted during the war, beginning with children's evacuation from areas judged to be vulnerable. Within three days of 1 September 1939 827,000 schoolchildren and 524,000 mothers with children under school age had been evacuated under the aegis of the government. This is and has been a topic for detailed educational and social studies. Caring for evacuees was considered a national service: 'Keep them happy, Keep them safe'.

The return home of many of them did not mean that evacuation ended. It continued at different times and in different places during most of the war. So, too, did the setting of fixed billeting allowances. Only after September 1944 did the process begin to stop. Evacuation had exposed social problems, including problems of communication, without solving them.

All children, whether evacuees or not, were expected, but not forced, to make their own contribution to the war effort in activities as various as collecting salvage, growing potatoes and serving in hospitals. They were told encouragingly that through their work they were helping to win the war. The organisation of their work was planned and supervised by schools and by voluntary organisations and, although in December 1941 the Board of Education decided to issue an Order that boys and girls over the age of 17 should register, no effort was made to force them to take up service below the age of 18. Children were still thought of as children. Nonetheless, a further registration of 16 year olds took place in 1944, and the 1941 Order was not revoked until December 1945.

Half of the children who registered were called to an interview, a cardinal point of the scheme. It was revealing that some of the girls interviewed were judged to be more in need of rest than work: they were

Above Working mothers needed their own mothers, other relatives or good neighbours to care for their children, which in this poster is accorded the status of a 'national service'. Only a few factories provided crèches.

Right 'The Riveting School', September 1941: Under guidance, these boys are in a shipyard learning a trade.

Left From a very early age children were called upon to advertise war savings. At the same time, war savings were advertised as being in the interests of children: they would underwrite the future.

expected by their families to do hours of unpaid housework after they had returned from hours of paid work. There had been an obvious incentive for them to take up factory work since in war conditions shortages of adult labour caused the wages of the under-16s to rise. The school leaving age was 14, and concern was expressed, not least by teachers (their numbers had fallen), both about the nature of some kinds of juvenile employment and about the effect of the relatively high wages paid to 'children' who were now being turned by order into 'young citizens'.

It was scarcely surprising that after the 1941 interviews had been held the number of boys and girls who went on to join a National Service body for the first time was disappointingly small. Donald and Marjorie Trust evaluated the registration positively in a pamphlet published at the time. Far-sighted, they believed that education was a life-long process, adding that 'only a perfectionist dare expect the generation which had registered to have the appetite and capacity for life-long education as we understand it'.

Right The life led by
'British Boy' – George
Metcalfe of Upper
Norwood, London – was
'typically that of British
youth in wartime… in his
rare leisure time George
visits the Ballet with his
girlfriend and goes
dancing, as boys all over
the world do'. A service
engineer in a factory that
made electro-acoustic
products, George was
called 'Micky' by his work
mates 'because when he
started work… his job
was chiefly connected
with microphones'.

Many boys and girls were, of course, already members of pre-National Service units
or youth clubs. Both the Boy Scout movement and the Girl Guides had official
histories published after the war. 'Good Turns' had 'multiplied prodigiously' during
six years of war. As early as December 1939, Girl Guides had launched a 'Save All
Supplies' scheme and Boy Scouts had 'helped invaluably' with evacuees, it was
claimed, erecting shelters during the Blitz and taking care to look after vulnerable
people who were sleeping in them. The Scouts of Bethnal Green had set up 5,000
three-tier bunks in the shelters, working in the evenings and at weekends.

Scouts collected 100,000 tons of waste paper, with the Cambridge troops gathering
201 tons in nine months. Kent troops broke all records: they collected 2,000 tons in
six months. Salisbury Scouts, responding to the slogan 'Rubbish Makes Rashers', had
collected 20 tons of pig food in one month. In the countryside Scouts spent over
2 million hours in harvesting and other farm work. In hospitals they were employed
as messengers and as telephone operators, cleaned wards and carried stretchers.
Thirteen troops in Croydon had been so actively involved in all hospital departments

that they became known as 'the Hospital Scouts'. Girl Guides cleaned jam jars as well as making jam itself. They specialised in cooking, including so-called 'Blitz cooking', but they also organised 'Grand Gift Weeks'. They preferred collecting all kinds of articles – from pans to wild plants – to growing vegetables.

Brownies worked closely with Guides but, like all young children, most of them – including the Wolf Cubs – preferred play to work. Even in wartime the old maxim, untinged by propaganda, prevailed: 'All Work and No Play Makes Jack a Dull Boy'. 'Colour your own barrage balloon' was one of the diversions suggested in the *British Boys' and Girls' War-time Play Book*.

Taking into account this rounded picture of children's wartime 'outside activities', it is necessary to relate it to what was going on in schools, where it proved difficult to maintain basic educational standards given the pressures of war and the absence of many teachers on war service. Through its school broadcasts, the BBC played a

Below Emptying fruit from picking baskets into bushel baskets ready for collection by lorries. In 1943, these Boy Scouts were at the very beginning of the jam production line.

Printed for H.M. Stationery Office by J. Howitt & Son Ltd., Nottingham. 51-4831

Above There were hints of all kinds, so many that it was difficult to take them all in. There was a parallel page of hints for boys that offered different incentives. When chocolate was restored, an advertisement for Mars Bars that showed a boy digging, told the boys that 'M Bs have to be won': 'Youngsters who salvage, dig and save for Victory deserve every encouragement.' The advertisement, placed at the end of some war-time Penguin paperbacks, also told parents to 'Let the kiddies know that, from now on, Mars are strictly reserved for work warranting the award of a Mars (for Merit) Bar.'

major part in making up for local deficiencies, but it was the teachers, some of them working on beyond normal retirement age, who kept the schools going, often in intimidating circumstances.

There were some changes in the curriculum. One photograph shows a class of 'young Britons' studying American history, too little studied (if at all) before the war. Another photograph from Dartington Hall in Devonshire, which had housed a pioneering experimental private school, showed evacuees learning to mend their own boots and shoes.

The future relationship between private ('public') schools and schools run by local education authorities was much discussed during the War, although it was deliberately not at the centre of R A Butler's Education Act of 1944, which reorganised 'state education', turning the Board of Education into a full Ministry and creating a new pattern of secondary education. Most important of all, it proposed raising the school-leaving age to 16.

Before the formation of Churchill's government, the old Board had begun to issue a sequence of memoranda on 'The Schools in Wartime' that covered many of the subjects dealt with in the various chapters of this book. Thus, the very first memorandum offered simple directives for 'digging', while memorandum No 7 (November 1939) was called 'Needle Subjects'. It described in its first paragraph an unnamed boy evacuee who, 'through no fault of his own', arrived 'insufficiently and unsuitably clad' and who 'after being properly fitted out' declared cheerfully that he had never had so many clothes in his life. Women's sewing parties and the Women's Voluntary Service had been hard at work.

The memorandum urged schools to arrange that girl evacuees, 'particularly the older ones', should do as much as they could for themselves and for their fellow evacuees. In some places it was suggested that where it was 'difficult to give the boys their usual forms of handiwork' they too might be initiated into the mysteries of knitting, darning, patching and fixing. 'We now have a golden opportunity to train the children to keep their clothes in good order and to take a pride in keeping a neat and tidy appearance.' The next memorandum was called 'Winter in the Garden'. Again it was focused on evacuees. One headmaster reported that a group of evacuated boys had dropped their tools where they stood after their gardening time was over. 'Tools should always be carefully cleaned and stacked tidily when the work is done.'

This was practical advice, not only for evacuees. A few months later, however, after many evacuees had returned home, garden hints ceased to refer to them, and the advice on offer was similar to that issued to gardeners everywhere, gardeners of all ages. What could have been more familiar than the words 'It is suggested that in newly developed school garden ground the chief crop grown should be the potato'? 'The nursery plot must have some protection from birds [which were very fond of young brassica plants]. The whole of a sowing is often taken as the result of one early morning visit by birds.'

Left The original caption for this 1942 picture was entitled 'East End Meets West End' and ran 'East End boys creating their own little miracle from heaps of rubble. Bethnal Green Bombed Sites Association arranged the land permits and provided the tools. A Boys Club did the training. Now the boys are transforming blitzed areas into allotments.'

Memorandum No 29 dealt with rabbit keeping. The Minister of Agriculture and Fisheries had asked for a great increase in the practice, and all schools, except perhaps (a pertinent 'perhaps') those in the centre of large towns, were therefore urged to consider seriously making 'this additional effort to contribute this extra bit to the Nation's Larder'. The memorandum suggested the formation of school rabbit clubs, similar to the poultry clubs it had dealt with in an earlier memorandum. It also recommended a reading list prepared by the British Rabbit Council and liaison with the National Federation of Young Farmers' Clubs.

On a very different subject, fuel economy, there were two memoranda. No 35, called 'The Battle for Fuel', linked fuel and food: 'Children should be reminded that there are kinds of food which are particularly helpful in producing warmth. Fats and starchy foods help to give us heat, so these should be used in larger amounts in winter than summer.' 'Potatoes may well be served two or three times a day.' 'Children need more syrup than adults.'

Memorandum No 37 consisted of an enterprising list of books, leaflets and films, including 'The Story of Coal' and 'How Gas is Made', and there was a demonstration chart 'From Coal Truck to Consumer'. In the Electricity Section there were lecture texts with slides on subjects as different as 'Michael Faraday – the Story of a Man who Changed the World' and 'Healing the Sick and Helping the Injured'. Lively children could be better informed about many aspects of work than their parents, most of whom were busy fighting or working.

Local education authorities varied as much as schools in how they responded to such memoranda. One active authority, East Suffolk, attracted an article in *Illustrated*: some were barely mentioned in local newspapers. The East Suffolk Youth Society mobilised squads, with their own leaders, to carry out village jobs of importance and persuaded a local farmer to lend them a horse and cart. The *Illustrated* writer praised the Copdock Squad, but drew a more general lesson. 'A spirit of determination, comradeship and loyalty', he believed, could galvanise children's efforts. 'A movement led by youth itself' could instil 'those ideals of responsibility, self-development and service that should be the aim of all who work in the cause of youth.'

While some young people were winning their laurels and well-deserved recognition, the contributions of old people to the war effort were not neglected in the press or by the Ministry of Information. Many of them were in close contact with the young members of their families if their sons and daughters were in the Forces or in war work.

There were others, men more than women, who were war workers themselves, including 700,000 old-age pensioners. They were among the people met by King George VI and Queen Elizabeth, when the King is reported to have asked Miles Thomas, Vice-Chairman of the great Nuffield organisation, 'Why is it I'm always introduced to the oldest worker? Wouldn't it be better if I met the youngest as a change?' On one

Below King George VI in military uniform stands over a young munitions worker at an un-named Royal Ordnance Factory in July 1940. Leonard Fiske was 15 years old and had started working in the factory only one day before. In the King's unannounced presence he never stopped working, feeding receiver bullets into his machine. The King had been welcomed to the factory by Herbert Morrison, then Minister of Supply, who introduced him 'smiling' to officials at the factory.

The Sword of Stalingrad

The battle of Stalingrad, a terrifying battle on both sides, began with a German attack on a tractor plant and ended with the German defeat and surrender. There were large numbers of dead and injured on both sides. At the end of the battle a Sword of Stalingrad was presented to Stalin by Churchill at the Teheran Conference, one of the series of war leaders' conferences, and Stalin kissed the scabbard. The sword, forged in a London factory by 83-year-old Tom Beasley, bore the words 'to the steel-tested citizens of Stalingrad, a gift from King George VI as a token of the homage of the British people'.

occasion, which was captured in a photograph reproduced here (*see* left), he did just that.

There was little awareness during the war that there would be a baby boom after it ended. Most of the talk was still of a declining population. Nor was there any clear intimation that there would be a post-war prolongation of life that would greatly increase the number of old-age pensioners at the end of the century. The problems of an ageing population were being discussed, but it was within a different demographic as well as social context.

There was one other basic contrast, this time between present and past rather than present and future. Far fewer servicemen lost their lives in the Second World War than during the First World War; not all of them had actually been fighting, and there was to be no sense this time, as there had been during the inter-war years, that a whole generation had been lost, an event without precedent in any previous war. After the first atomic bombs had been dropped on Hiroshima and Nagasaki in August 1945 it was evident that the whole world might be destroyed. Psychologically, that was as big a break as the war itself. But first came victory against the Germans, and when the atom bombs fell on Japan later in the year it seemed at the time to most people that they had hastened the timing of the second victory.

Above Old-age pensioners usually worked near their homes – in country or in city. Three 'veterans' in the North East – their average age was 71 – were employed in a factory that produced tanks.

Yorkshire Lad of 73 Gets BEM

This was the headline in local and national newspapers in January 1943 when Harry Hargreaves of Micklethwaite, near Bingley, was one of 82 workers given British Empire Medals. He operated a centre lathe in a factory making machine tools, vital in war production. He was said to have one 'etiquette problem' when he went to Buckingham Palace to receive his award. Could he wear clogs?

Out of
Battledress
... into

**MOSS
BROS**
& CO. LTD.

COVENT GARDEN
LONDON

VICTORY
AT LAST

Victory in 1945 is usually described in terms of nostalgic images: VE Day street parties; impressive military parades; members of the royal family waving from the balcony of Buckingham Palace. At a deeper level, however, as this book shows, it must be examined in the context both of British pre-war history, what had happened before, and of world history after 1945: what would come next.

Before the end of the war, a *Picture Post* article on a war artist who dealt in powerful personal images, Stanley Spencer ('Bending the Keel Plate'; 'Welders'), began with the sentence '"Advance!" – "Retreat" – "Surrender" – "Victory"'. The war words grow bigger and bigger in the headlines.' The last word 'victory' figured literally and metaphorically in agriculture – 'The Victory Harvest'. It also figured as early as 1941 in the BBC's *Music While You Work*, which introduced the slogan 'Victory through Harmony'. On the screen, *British Movietone News*, 'now showing' in 1943, was advertised with the words 'Nearer Victory. 1943 Success – Capitulation of Italy – 1944 Hitler?' There had been a 'V-campaign', launched in January 1941 on the Belgian Service of the BBC: it was felt to have come too soon.

It was in 1941, before 'the tide of war' had turned in favour of the Allies, that Keith Hancock, then Professor of History at Birmingham University, had been approached by Sir Edward Bridges, the Secretary of the War Cabinet, to edit official war histories. 'Was there any use or point in starting to write the history of war before we had won it?' Hancock asked, not surprisingly, to which Bridges replied that he must 'think in long term of the continuity of the State and the advantages of funding our wartime experience for further use'.

This book has not hitherto mentioned the war work of civil servants, many of them temporary civil servants, a high proportion of them university professors and lecturers who worked long office hours while trying to keep in touch with their peacetime academic work. There was also an influx of women civil servants, working at all levels except the top. Their numbers more than doubled. One of them, employed as an Assistant Principal in the Treasury from 1942 until 1944, was the future novelist Iris Murdoch.

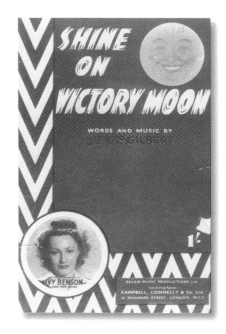

Above Many wartime song titles look backward to love enjoyed in the past and forward to still happier times. 'It's a lovely day tomorrow,' sang Vera Lynn, 'Tomorrow is a lovely day.'

After the war many civil servants, men and women behind the scenes, recorded their experiences, some of them dealing with matters of production and supply. Thus, Richard Pares, editor of the *English Historical Review*, wrote a chapter on his experiences as a production priorities officer in a book edited by another wartime civil servant working in the Cabinet Office, D N Chester, subsequently Warden of Nuffield College, Oxford. They thought that they had something to communicate for posterity, and their book was called *Lessons of the British War Economy* (1951). Oliver Franks, who after the war was Provost of two different Oxford colleges, with an ambassadorship to the United States in between, lectured at the highest level on his wartime experiences in the Ministry of Supply. The war had elevated him into the position of a major public servant, a term that carried with it prestige, as well as

influence. Meanwhile, the wife of a great public servant who preceded him, Cyril (Lord) Radcliffe, had been working in a munitions factory.

Some wartime civil servants became post-war politicians, among them Hugh Gaitskell and Harold Wilson, who were to be chosen as party leaders. There was to be continuity there, as Noel Annan explained in his book *Our Age* (1990), which concentrated on people who went to universities between the end of the First World War and 1951, six years after the Second World War. This was not only a Census Year, when it was possible to compare pre-war and post-war figures, but also the year of the Festival of Britain.

Universities, which along with the press did much to set the mood, found it difficult to return to normal in 1945. Parts of many of them had been used for non-

Above Whatever public celebrations of victory, local or national, there might have been – and there were many, of all kinds – it was registered more intimately (if still with flags) in private welcomes to returning servicemen.

academic purposes during the war when student numbers fell sharply. Some universities, however, like Sheffield, were proud of their war record. Its specific war contributions, whether made by single persons or teams, were listed at Sheffield by the chemist Dr Brynmor Jones, who was to play a significant part 20 years later, as Vice-Chancellor of Hull University, in the planning of the Open University. One Sheffield example that he gave was that of students in the Department of Metallurgy and a number of members of staff voluntarily working three shifts a day in 1940, heat-testing forgings for steel helmets (45,000 of them) and for tank parts.

Post-1945 became a time for businesses, as well as for individuals and for universities, to look back over the experiences of the war and 'the last lap to peace', while they were fresh; and sometimes they chose well-known authors to write what were usually brief histories to set alongside the official war histories. Thus, *Ford at War* (1946), describing the story of Dagenham ('bombs falling: production rising') was written by Hilary St George Saunders, author of *The Battle of Britain* (1941), *Bomber Command* (1941) and *Combined Operations* (1943), as well as of the wartime history of the Middlesex Hospital and the Boy Scout movement. Saunders was a one-man Hancock team in himself. One of the illustrations in his history showed a tank rolling

Below Returning to 'civvy street' meant a return to civilian clothes. The clothing industry was ready to supply 'demob suits' for men and other basic items of clothing for both sexes. The depots where they were 'issued' were less interested in individual taste than in getting large numbers of people through their doors and 'into the world' as quickly as possible.

down Regent Street for one of the Ford Company's wartime exhibitions. These were attended by over 900,000 people.

Morgan's at War, 1939–1945 (1946), sub-titled 'A Story of Achievement Under Fire', talked of war factories as 'industrial garrisons'. It included photographs of some of 'the men who stayed at their jobs' and of 'the women who came to help', along with 'thumbnail sketches' of a number of them. There had been 'one girl who came back': Mrs Andrews, who during the First World War had operated a Morgan crane, 'driving it out high above the River Thames to pick up supplies of raw materials for the factory from the barges below'. In 1939 she returned and did the same job all over again.

In 1945 women, and men, were returning from war jobs to peacetime jobs at the same time as people serving in the Forces were being demobilised. Even before they collected their gratuities and put on their 'demob suits', symbols of status changes, they were offered a wide variety of training schemes, as well as being warned to beware of 'sharks' who might 'trick them out of their gratuities'.

The courses, some of them correspondence courses, varied from accountancy to bricklaying. The latter, it was suggested, would be of great national use too. There was considerable publicity too about prefabricated houses largely made from aluminium alloy. They were being built in 'a British aircraft factory which produced the RAF Beaufighter'. On a bombed site outside Selfridges store in Oxford Street, not far from the place where Woolton visited the wartime Potato Fair (*see* p57), a lightweight aluminium house, factory-made in four sections, was on public display.

WHAT CAN YOU DO IN CIVVY ST.?

ARMY EDUCATION SCHEME
WILL PREPARE YOU FOR YOUR RETURN TO CIVIL LIFE

Above Education, which had been much discussed in wartime, offered one route, or rather a number of routes, into the future. Posters were used to set out the choices.

Post-war Training and Retraining

In 1945 continuing emphasis was being placed on the need for training and retraining. The heading of one semi-official statement then read, 'The untrained man can help himself and the country at the same time'… by entering a Training Centre.

The statement gave details of 'types' of entrants, not of particular individuals, and went on to describe a recent six-month course in engineering, where the age range had run from 18 to 45 or older. Some of the men were from the 'special areas', parts of the country with heavy pre-war unemployment, which had been designated as such during the 1930s, but which had 'recovered' during the war. They had found 'skill and hope' in the centres as the recovery proceeded.

For the author of the statement the courses with a high pass rate were not 'the result of the sudden transition created by war' or by its ending. They had been developed through 'years of thought and experience'. Out of every 100 entrants, 92 found jobs in industry. Some of them had succeeded in passing a 'placing test' before the six months were over. This was 'a great sociological experiment'. Training schemes multiplied with demobilisation. They were associated with a variety of educational establishments, including newly-founded Army Formation Colleges.

Much was made not only of its materials ('RAF returns her Aluminium to the Housewife', *see* below) but, of the fact that all its fittings were 'electrical'. Far away in the mines, coalminers were being photographed driving bulldozers imported from the United States. At a training centre in Sheffield they were being 'taught to become skilled mechanics and electricians'. An increased use of electricity in mine, factory and home was being considered as an indicator of 'modernisation'. One symbol of 'modernisation' was the synthetic nylon stocking. British 'Victory Stockings', in Utility styles, were to pass quickly from the scene.

Right Aluminium, enthusiastically collected for salvage in 1940 and 1941, was hailed as a wonder metal in 1945, capable of use in a wide variety of ways. Here it is being returned to a mundane use: 'Five years after Britain's appeal to housewives to surrender their saucepans for conversion into aircraft parts… aircraft parts were being reconverted into saucepans.'

R.A.F. Returns her Aluminium to the Housewife

FIVE YEARS AFTER BRITAIN'S APPEAL to housewives to surrender their saucepans for conversion into aircraft parts (see page 384, Vol. 3), aircraft parts were being reconverted into saucepans. At a London factory in January 1946 a 30-cwt. tilting furnace (1) was being used for melting down R.A.F. airscrews. Ingots, remelted, are being poured into moulds (2) from which the finished lids (3) are removed. This polisher (4) wears a protective mask. Pans are carefully scrutinized (5) before being assembled (6). PAGE 628

There was another 'mighty switch': from tanks to peacetime cars, hailed by Miles Thomas, who quickly became the post-war spokesman of the 'motor car industry'. The government placed hope in automobiles for export. As many people at home had learnt to drive cars, demand for them was now as marked – or so Thomas put it – as the demand for tanks had been in 1940. 'The industry is looking forward to the day when, instead of the 1939 figure of one car to every twenty-five of the population, we approach the American ratio of one in five.' His enthusiasm was unambiguous: 'Think what that would mean in increased employment.'

Transformation to Peace at Woolwich Arsenal

FIVE OF OUR LARGEST ROYAL ORDNANCE FACTORIES—at Woolwich, Cardiff, Hayes (Middlesex), Nottingham and Patricroft, near Manchester—in the early winter of 1945 received Government orders to switch some of their space from gun and tank manufacture to peacetime production. At the Royal Gun and Carriage Factory, Woolwich, which has 2,000 employees, mechanics assembled motor-lorries for shipment to Europe as the last 6-pounder anti-tank gun left the shop (1). Here, also, thousands of railway wagons, some over 40 years old, were being reconditioned (3) for service abroad, while workmen cleared away the ammunition boxes and gun-barrel cases. At a Walthamstow, London, aircraft factory finishing touches were given to a Mosquito as cabinet-makers assembled Utility-type wardrobes (2). See also page 558.
Photos 1 and 3 Exclusive to THE WAR ILLUSTRATED ; *2, Associated Press*   PAGE 554

Left In the early winter of 1945, five of the country's largest Royal Ordnance factories – at Woolwich, Cardiff, Hayes, Nottingham and Partricroft, near Manchester – received government orders to switch some of their space from gun and tank manufacture to peacetime production. At the Royal Gun and Carriage Factory, Woolwich, which had 2,000 employees, mechanics can be seen assembling lorries for shipment to Europe as the last six-pounder anti-tank gun leaves the workshop.

J B Priestley, who throughout the war had urged servicemen to 'look ahead', was already unsure as to whether such visions were healthy. In a 1940 radio *Postscript* he had unfolded his own vision:

> *It may be possible yet, even while we struggle and endure, and at last batter our way through to victory, to achieve what's long been overdue in this island, and, that is, not only to retain what's best out of an old tradition, but to increase that heritage by raising at last the quality of our life.*

An unlikely partner, *Vogue* magazine, took a similar line in June 1945, looking back over the war years and trying to list 'what we want to keep, what we want to get rid of, and what we want to have back'.

Under the first heading it focused on 'a busy and prosperous countryside and the feeling for the land learnt by some evacuees and landgirls'. Under the last came 'Flowers in our flowerbeds, and cabbage banished to its proper place out of sight and out of smell'. And *Vogue* too had another unlikely partner of its own, very different from Priestley, Mr Middleton (*see* p.58), who now admitted that vegetables bored him and that he could never 'love an onion where a dahlia might grow'.

It was not Mr Middleton's dahlia, however, that was picked out as the flower of peace, but the lily of the valley. The fruit of peace, the banana, came from abroad. A notice issued by the Covent Garden Market Wholesalers' Distribution Committee in October 1945 announced that 'the Ministry of Food have authorised the importation of bananas' and that business firms with 'Banana Rooms' in the market should 'approach the Committee at once'. Green bananas could be heated by gas in the Banana Rooms and ripened in five or six days. Meanwhile on the Clyde, banana boats were being 'refurbished in readiness for the resumption of the trade with Jamaica and the Cameroons'. Globalisation again, but not quite the finish of Austerity.

It would take time for the latter to come to an end, and most people understood this. But a leader in *The Listener* in May suggested that 'things will be better than they were in the twenties' for two reasons. First, many civilians had shared the soldiers' dangers, second, neither soldiers nor civilians would begin the peace with the 'exaggerated hopes' of 1918. This did not rule out Hope itself.

'The New Britain Must Be Built on Coal'

"Here you are! Don't lose it again!"

Selected Further Reading

The best introduction to the themes and content of this book is A Marwick, *Britain in a Century of Total War: War, Peace and Social Change* (1968). For a different perspective J Keegan, *The Battle for History, Refighting World War II* (1996). See also M Gilbert, *Second World War* (1989); and M Howard, 'Total War in the Twentieth Century' in B Bond and I Roy (eds), *War and Society, A Year Book of Military History* (1979). P Hennessy, *Never Again, Britain 1945–1951* (1992) is a study based on interviews.

There is a huge anthology of comment on the War, personal and otherwise, edited by D Flower and J Reeves, *The War* (1960). For the fullest history of the War in all its aspects, A Calder, *The People's War* (1969) is outstanding. For the politics see P Addison, *The Road to 1945* (1975) and K Jefferys, *The Churchill Coalition and War-time Politics* (1991). For the economics see, J M Winter (ed), *War and Economic Development* (1975); A S Milward, *War, Economy and Society, 1939–1945* (1977); and C Barnett, *The Audit of War* (1986).

Six relevant biographies are A Bullock, *The Life and Times of Ernest Bevin*, Vol II, *Minister of Labour, 1940–1945* (1967); J Harris, *William Beveridge* (2nd edn 1997); M Gilbert, *The Churchill Biography*, Vol VI, *Finest Hour, 1939–1941* (1983); K Harris, *Attlee* (1982); B Donoughue and G W Jones, *Herbert Morrison, Portrait of a Politician* (1973); S Burgess, *Stafford Cripps* (1999).

The official war histories include W K Hancock and M M Gowing, *British War Economy* (1949); R Titmuss, *Problems of Social Policy*; W H B Court, *Coal* (1951); R J Hammond, *Food*, 2 Vols (1951, 1956);

M Postan, *British War Production* (1952); J Hurstfield, *The Control of Raw Materials* (1953); P Inman, *Labour in the Munitions Industries* (1987); W Hornby, *Factories and Plant* (1958); C I Savage, *Inland Transport* (1957); C Behrens, *Merchant Shipping and the Demands of War* (1955); and H M D Parker, *Manpower: A Study of Wartime Policy and Administration* (1957). See also V S Pritchett, *Build the Ship* (1946); Ian Hay, ROF, *The Story of the Royal Ordnance Factories, 1939–1948* (1949); P H J Gosden, *Education* (1992); M Gowing, *Britain and Atomic Energy, 1939–1945* (1964); and C H Woddington, *Operational Research in World War 2* (1973).

For the Home Front see N Longmate, *How We Lived Then* (1971), Susan Briggs, *Keep Smiling Through* (1975); A Marwick, *The Home Front: The British and the Second World War* (1976); and H L Smith (ed), *War and Social Change: British Society in the Second World War* (1982).

For the Women's Land Army see I Tillett, *The Cinderella Army* (1988); B Powell and N Westmacott, *The Women's Land Army* (1997); and G Huxley, *Lady Denman* (1962).

For comparisons with Britain see M J Harris, F D Mitchell and S J Schechter, *The Home Front: America During World War II* (1984); R Polenberg (ed), *America at War: The Home Front, 1941–1945* (1968); J Hakim, *A History of the United States, Peace and All That Jazz* (1995); T Charman, *The German Home Front, 1939–1945* (1989); R J Overy, *War and Economy in the Third Reich* (1994); M Harrison, *The Soviet Home Front, 1941–1945* (1991).

For communication, propaganda and entertainment see A Briggs, *The War of Words* (1970); S Nicholas, *The Echo of War, Home Front Propaganda and the Wartime BBC* (1996); I McLaine, *Ministry of Morale: Home Front Morale and the Ministry of Information in World War II* (1979); M Balfour, *Propaganda in War, 1939–1945: Organisations, Policies and Publics in Britain and Germany* (1979); A C H Smith, *Paper Voices: The Popular Press and Social Change, 1935–1965* (1975); T Hopkinson (ed), *'Picture Post', 1938–1950* (1970); J Darracott and B Loftus, *Second World War Posters* (1985); K R M Short (ed), *Film and Radio Propaganda in World War II* (1983); T Aldgate and J Richards, *Britain Can Take It, The British Cinema in the Second World War* (1994 edn); P M Taylor (ed), *Britain and the Cinema in the Second World War* (1989).

For memoirs see N Last, *Nella Last's War: a Mother's Diary* (1983); A Calder and D Sheridan (eds), *Speak for Yourself: A Mass Observation Anthology, 1937–1949* (1984); Mass Observation, *People in Production* (1942) and *War Factory* (1944); D Sheridan, *Wartime Women: An Anthology of Women's War-time Writing for Mass Observation* (1991); P Summerfield, *Women Workers in the Second World War, Production and Patriarchy in Conflict* (1989); D Agnew, *Bevin Boy* (1947); A P Rowe, *The Story of Radar* (1948); R W Clark, *The Rise of the Boffins* (1962).

For the last chapter in this book see Mass Observation, *The Journey Home* (1944); P Reese, *Home Coming Heroes* (1992); D N Chester (ed), *Lessons of the British War Economy* (1951); M Sisson and P French (eds), *The Age of Austerity* (1963); H Hopkins, *The New Look* (1963).

Index

Author's acknowledgements

I would like to express my gratitude for the expert help given me by Terry Charman and Christopher Dowling at the Imperial War Museum, and for the co-operation and invaluable support of Margaret Little and Stephen Guise at Mitchell Beazley. I also owe a personal debt, as always, to Pat Spencer, who dealt patiently and efficiently with my various drafts. This is a book that has been heartening to write, and I am solely responsible, of course, for its contents.

Asa Briggs